12 00

Penguin
LIVES

In Memory of

LOLA JOHNSON

BY

STUART JEAN MATTSON
&
GENE FOUGNER

*ONE OF THE FIRST AFRO
AMERICANS IN
PRESCOTT VALLEY.

Rosa Parks

A LIPPER / VIKING BOOK

American Heritage History of the United States

*The Unfinished Presidency: Jimmy Carter's Journey
Beyond the White House*

John F. Kennedy and Europe (ed.)

*Witness to America: An Illustrated Documentary History
of the United States from the Revolution to Today*
(ed., with Stephen E. Ambrose, Henry Steele Commager,
and Allan Nevins)

Rise to Globalism: American Foreign Policy Since 1939
(with Stephen E. Ambrose), eighth edition

Dean Acheson and the Making of U.S. Foreign Policy (ed.)

Jean Monnet: Path to European Unity (ed.)

The Majic Bus: An American Odyssey

Dean Acheson: The Cold War Years, 1953–1971

Driven Patriot: The Life and Times of James Forrestal
(with Townsend Hoopes)

FDR and the Creation of the U.N.

DOUGLAS BRINKLEY

Rosa Parks

A Penguin Life

A LIPPER / VIKING BOOK

VIKING
Published by the Penguin Group
Penguin Putnam Inc., 375 Hudson Street,
New York, New York 10014, U.S.A.
Penguin Books Ltd, 27 Wrights Lane, London W8 5TZ, England
Penguin Books Australia Ltd, Ringwood, Victoria, Australia
Penguin Books Canada Ltd, 10 Alcorn Avenue,
Toronto, Ontario, Canada M4V 3B2
Penguin Books (N.Z.) Ltd, 182–190 Wairau Road,
Auckland 10, New Zealand

Penguin Books Ltd, Registered Offices:
Harmondsworth, Middlesex, England

First published in 2000 by Viking Penguin,
a member of Penguin Putnam Inc.

1   3   5   7   9   10   8   6   4   2

Grateful acknowledgment is made for permission to reprint the following copy-
righted works:
"Rosa" from On the Bus with Rosa Parks by Rita Dove. Copyright © 1999 by Rita
Dove. Used by permission of W. W. Norton & Company, Inc.
Excerpts from Rosa Parks: My Story by Rosa Parks with Jim Haskins. Copyright ©
Rosa Parks, 1992. Used by permission of Dial Books, a member of Penguin Putnam
Books for Young Readers.

LIBRARY OF CONGRESS CATALOGING IN PUBLICATION DATA
Brinkley, Douglas.
Rosa Parks / Douglas Brinkley.
p.   cm.—(Penguin lives series)
"A Lipper/Viking book."
ISBN 0-670-89160-6
1. Parks, Rosa, 1913–Juve.   2. Afro-American women civil rights workers—
Alabama—Montgomery—Biography.   3. Civil rights workers—
Alabama—Montgomery—Biography.   4. Afro-Americans—Civil rights—
Alabama—Montgomery—History—20th century   5. Segregation in transportation—
Alabama—Montgomery—History—20th century   6. Montgomery (Ala.)—
Race relations.   7. Montgomery (Ala.)—Biography.   I. Title.   II. Series.
F334.M753P373 2000
323'.092—dc21   00–035916

This book is printed on acid-free paper.
∞

Printed in the United States of America
Set in Goudy
Designed by Francesca Belanger

For Johnnie Mae Carr, H. H. Leonards,
Maura Pierce, and Elaine Eason Steele . . .
the modern-day embodiments of
the women in Mark 14:8—
"She hath done what she could. . . ."

How she sat there,
the time right inside a place
so wrong it was ready.

That trim name with
its dream on a bench
to rest on. Her sensible coat.

Doing nothing was the doing:
the clean flame of her gaze
carved by a camera flash.

How she stood up
when they bent down to retrieve
her purse. That courtesy.

—Rita Dove
"Rosa" from *On the Bus with Rosa Parks* (1999)

Trails of troubles,
Roads of battles,
Paths of victory
We shall walk.

—Bob Dylan
"Paths of Victory" (1964)

CONTENTS

Prologue

In quietness and in confidence shall be your strength.

—Isaiah 30:15

OF ALL THE CIVIL RIGHTS SITES worthy of pilgrimage in Alabama, and there are many, none transfixes the historical imagination quite like that marked only by a simple green sign on an ordinary-looking street in Montgomery. The sensation comes from something that happened there, not from the street itself, though it has a history of its own that adds to the resonance of the event. During the War Between the States it was a bumpy thoroughfare known as Plank Road, after some progress-minded Montgomerians applied to it the Russian method of smoothing muddy lanes by laying planks of wood across them—which worked fine in the icy tundra but proved useless in the American South, where summer's swelter rotted the wood into mush. In the late 1880s the road was renamed in honor of New York's Grover Cleveland, the first post–Civil War U.S. president to visit Montgomery; it was paved at the turn of the century when the initial generation of gasoline-powered automobiles came chugging into town. Not that many did: Montgomery was essentially a railroad and riverboat outpost, and through the first half of the twen-

1

tieth century Cleveland Avenue remained an unremarkable road in an average city in the Deep South.

That changed on December 1, 1955, when Rosa Louise Parks, a prim, bespectacled, forty-two-year-old mulatto seamstress, made history by refusing to give up her seat on the Cleveland Avenue bus to a white man. Her courageous act touched off a 381-day boycott of the city's bus system, led by Dr. Martin Luther King, Jr., and is now considered the beginning of the American civil rights movement. As Eldridge Cleaver, author of *Soul on Ice,* noted of that winter day: "Somewhere in the universe, a gear in the machinery shifted." Within a year after the Montgomery bus boycott, forty-two other local movements were organized in the South to combat racial segregation. From that day onward, the phrase "back of the bus" became a synonym for, and a rallying cry against, racial discrimination. And to many backward thinkers, Rosa Parks became a pariah: In the aftermath of her intransigence, she received a barrage of death threats. Yet she continued to reside at the Cleveland Courts housing project, in a poor part of town known as Peacock Tract, with her barber husband, Raymond Parks, and her mother, Leona Edwards McCauley, in shoebox-sized apartment 634.

Old-timers say that the two-story, redbrick housing project, built in 1941, was a decent place to live when the Parks family resided there from 1951 to 1957. It was a segregated community center of sorts, where Montgomery's African Americans could gather for Saturday barbecues in the grassy courtyard, then proceed the following morning in their Sunday best to their choice of nearby Lutheran or Baptist or African Methodist Episcopal (AME) churches to praise the holy gospel and the everlasting joy of Jesus Christ. "We all pulled for each other at Cleveland Courts," Parks recalled. "We all loved Jesus and despised Jim Crow."

That was then. Four decades later, Cleveland Courts had soured into a decrepit eyesore, strewn with the leavings of discarded lives and surrounded by piles of garbage. The complex had turned into a squalid, half-living monument to the failure of Lyndon B. Johnson's War on Poverty, fronting onto a street of vacant lots choked with weeds and broken bottles, a preying ground for crack dealers and prostitutes. All too often the still night at Cleveland Courts is pierced by random bursts of gunfire and the eventual wailing of ambulances sent to pick up the latest casualties of the gang wars.

The simple green sign that marks the once-muddy street and haunts the soul reads: Rosa L. Parks Avenue.

But for all its grinding poverty, violence, and despair, there is still something uplifting about Rosa L. Parks Avenue. Just a block from Cleveland Courts, at the corner where Mosley's Meat World offers Collard Greens for 99 Cents and Fresh Pork Spareribs for $1.49/lb., Rosa L. Parks Avenue intersects West Jeff Davis Avenue, named for the only president of the short-lived Confederate States of America, who was inaugurated at Montgomery's state capitol in 1861. There, where the two roads meet, black people and white people pass by in their cars, headed to the same restaurants, swimming pools, high schools, and public libraries. And that simple, mundane sight makes it clear that even with all its crime and destitution, things are better in Montgomery than they used to be. Jefferson Davis's Dixie and George Wallace's Jim Crow are long gone, supplanted by Rosa Parks as the enduring symbol of a more tolerant New South and a more civilized America. As Taylor Branch put it in his Pulitzer Prize–winning history

Parting the Waters: America in the King Years, 1954–1963, Parks's "character represented one of the isolated high blips on the graph of human nature, offsetting a dozen or so sociopaths."

Parks's fearless act of civil disobedience in 1955—her emphatic refusal to budge, on principle—gave credence to novelist Ralph Ellison's claim that after three hundred years of white domination, African Americans had learned they could take the "headwhipping" and still maintain their dignity no matter how brutal the blows. Caribbean historian C. L. R. James, writing to a friend in March 1957, called Parks's intransigence "revolutionary . . . profoundly so," comparable to Kwame Nkrumah's successful independence movement in Ghana that same year and to the dashed Hungarian uprising against Soviet totalitarianism the year before. "Here is something that is new," James wrote of the Montgomery bus boycott that predated them both. "It's one of the most astonishing events in the history of the human struggle." The Czech Republic's Václav Havel deemed Parks a "sustainable hero" simply because "when her time came she sat down." Indeed, in the spring of 1989, when a lone Chinese student stood defiantly before an army tank in Beijing's Tiananmen Square as hundreds of millions of people watched around the world, it was, as South African president Nelson Mandela put it, "a Rosa Parks moment."

Novelist Richard Wright's posthumously published *American Hunger* anguished over the "paradoxical Negro" who was "an organized part of the nation" yet "excluded by the entire tide and direction of American culture." By 1999, however, Rosa Parks had clearly smashed through that exclusion: Mainstream America embraced the seamstress from the projects as a national treasure, an icon made flesh. Everyone, it seemed, wanted to pay homage to the octogenarian Parks as the twentieth century drew to a close. *Time* magazine proclaimed Parks one of the hundred most significant individuals of the century, noting that her "modesty" and "serenely human" bravery made her unique among global heroes. Her status as an unimpeachable heroine even for a cynical age was cemented when she was asked to sit next to First Lady Hillary Rodham Clinton at the last State of the Union Address of the American Century, delivered by Bill Clinton the same week the U.S. Senate was deliberating whether to impeach him. It was for moral support that the president asked Rosa Parks to sit in the gallery next to the First Lady, and the legend delivered: The mere mention of her name inspired the longest and loudest applause of the night. A few weeks later, after celebrating a mass in St. Louis on what would likely be his last visit to the United States, Pope John Paul II met with and blessed Rosa Parks, hanging a long white rosary around her neck in recognition of her Christian contribution to humanity. "My life-time mission has been simple," she wrote the pontiff in deep gratitude but also concerned about sexism in the Catholic Church, "that all men *and* women are created equal under the eyes of our Lord." Around the same time, former U.S. poet laureate Rita Dove published *On the Bus with Rosa Parks*, a tribute to the emblematic everywoman who changed her nation by "sitting there / waiting for the moment to take her."

That Rosa Parks deserves to be remembered as the "Mother of the Civil Rights Movement" is beyond dispute. Yet as the historian Deborah Gray White argues in *Too Heavy a Load: Black Women in Defense of Themselves, 1894–1994*,

Parks was by no means the first of her race and gender to challenge racial-segregation laws on a public transportation system. In 1884, Ida B. Wells, a Memphis newspaperwoman both renowned and reviled for her crusade against lynching, balked when asked to move from her seat in a "white only" railway car and had to be physically evicted from it by three white men. Wells sued the railroad and won, only to have the Tennessee State Supreme Court overturn the verdict. Similarly, Charlotte Hawkins Brown, president of the North Carolina Federation of Women's Clubs from 1915 to 1936, sued the railroad after being ejected from a Pullman berth on a train passing near Anniston, Alabama. Brown won a small settlement but found her triumph scant recompense, disgusted that "inconveniencing a Negro woman or humiliating her, in the eyes of the court, was never considered as any great outrage on personality." Even in Montgomery itself, the same year Parks was arrested, three other African-American women had refused to move from their bus seats, but their cases went nowhere.

So what made Rosa Parks and her civil disobedience different? "Ella Baker, Fannie Lou Hamer, even Angela Davis didn't have that biblical quality, which made Rosa Parks a saint, someone divine," explained James Farmer, founder of the Congress of Racial Equality. "There was a strange religious glow about Rosa—a kind of humming Christian light, which gave her a unique majesty." In the opinion of historian Henry Louis Gates, Jr., it was that Rosa Parks seemed to be the "Harriet Tubman of our time." Tubman, of course, was the best-known conductor of the Underground Railroad; as a fugitive slave living in Philadelphia, she made at least fifteen forays across the Mason-Dixon line to personally deliver more than two hundred slaves to freedom. Dubbed "the Moses of her people," Tubman lived well into her nineties, witnessing the advent of the Automobile Age. Gates claims it was through "Providence" that Rosa Parks was born in February 1913, a month before Harriet Tubman died. "Her death," Gates has written, "suggests that she could not leave this world until she had been assured that she would have a successor and a replacement."

Other historians like to point out the striking similarities between Rosa Parks and Mahatma Gandhi. It turns out that Gandhi steeled his resolve to fight for social justice in 1893 when, traveling to Johannesburg in a first-class train compartment, he was ordered to move to the "colored" cars in the rear. When he refused, he was hauled off the train and left to spend the night in a freezing railway station. Later that same trip, he was beaten by a white stagecoach driver and refused entry into various "European Only" hotels. In addition, both the seamstress Parks and the weaver Gandhi—who spent a few hours at his spinning wheel every day—believed that sewing cultivated inner strength; and both ascetics were, of course, arrested for acts of civil disobedience, although Gandhi spent 2,338 days in prison and Parks just two hours in jail. Still, leading politicians of their respective days saw Gandhi and Parks as equally dangerous agitators: Winston Churchill scorned the former as a "half-naked fakir stirring up sedition," while the latter was labeled a "nigger traitor" by half of the Democrats in the U.S. Senate from south of the Mason-Dixon line. Finally, both activists led by example, Parks embracing Gandhi's maxim: "Action is my domain. It's not what I say but what I do that matters."

Some scholars have argued that the closest historical

precursor to Rosa Parks is the former slave and itinerant preacher Sojourner Truth, born Isabella Baumfree, who from 1832 to 1883 crisscrossed the northern United States advocating first the abolition of slavery and then the cause of women's rights. Not that the two had much in common: Truth was a dazzling orator who thrilled congregations with her own bold and pithy gospel, most famously in her 1851 "And Ain't I a Woman" speech challenging a chauvinistic minister's claim that because Jesus had been a man, only men had a claim to human rights. Parks espoused the same beliefs in equal rights for all but was Truth's exact opposite in demeanor: shy, self-effacing, soft-spoken, and averse to crowds. Yet they shared a few crucial qualities, too; both women were deeply Christian from childhood, expressed themselves in biblically rich metaphors, and had an almost mystical effect on nearly everyone they came in contact with. More concretely, Truth won renown for testing Washington, D.C.'s streetcar antidiscrimination law after the Civil War; Parks, for desegregating Montgomery, Alabama's bus system. "The people I wish I had been taught more about in high school were Sojourner Truth and Harriet Tubman," Parks wrote an inquiring high school history class. "They both exemplified a Godly spirit, self-determination, and a willingness to make any sacrifice necessary to free African Americans from slavery."

Neither Parks nor Truth were natural writers—the latter, in fact, was illiterate—but the two managed to dictate similarly uplifting autobiographies, *The Narrative of Sojourner Truth* and *Rosa Parks: My Story*.

My Story offers the best available chronology of Parks's life, as no biography has been written about her until now.

Happily, the ghostwriter—Alabama native Jim Haskins, author of biographies of such other notable African Americans as the composer Scott Joplin and Congresswoman Barbara Jordan—crafted a fine autobiography out of his many hours of tape-recorded interviews with Parks. Although the resulting memoir aims at young readers with a message about the power of Christian commitment in a world full of evil and hate groups like the Ku Klux Klan, *My Story* also chronicles some of the largely unknown details of its subject's life presented here. For example, the book shows Parks growing up in the piney woods of rural Alabama; working with various NAACP youth groups; struggling to help save the Scottsboro Boys (eight young black men sentenced to death in 1931 after their convictions, on concocted evidence, for the rapes of two white women on a freight train in Alabama); serving as secretary of the Montgomery chapter of the NAACP and at the organization's Alabama State Conferences through the 1940s and 1950s; forging a friendship with Dr. Martin Luther King, Jr.; and putting in twenty-three years as a legislative aide to Democratic congressman John Conyers of Michigan. What *My Story* doesn't do, or try to, is explain *why* Rosa Parks emerged as such a potent human symbol of freedom around the world.

Rosa Parks's bold act that December day in Montgomery, Alabama, has become legendary; and in the shadow of that legend, there is an unfortunate tendency to ignore the full story of her life as a civil rights activist, which began long before the day she just said no on the Cleveland Avenue bus and continued long after. Yet it remains unclear why Parks chose the particular evening of December 1, 1955, to refuse to relinquish her seat. Was she simply fed up after years of submitting to hundreds of such unfair demands? Was it because other African Americans had been arrested—and one man shot to death—for disobeying bus drivers that year? Had the NAACP put her up to it? Had she been brainwashed at the workshop on nonviolent resistance taught by radical activist Myles Horton that she had attended at the Highlander Folk School in August 1955? Was it that America's temper had changed the year before, when the U.S. Supreme Court declared school segregation unconstitutional in the *Brown v. Board of Education* case in May 1954? Did she make her stand because an all-white jury had just acquitted two of the suspected murderers of Emmett Till, a black fourteen-year-old who had been lynched in Mississippi that August for whistling at a white woman? Or was it just that Rosa Parks was physically tired that December day?

*What historians—myself included—refer to as the Montgomery bus "boycott" was called a "protest" by its African-American participants. During the reign of Jim Crow, boycotts were illegal in Alabama.

CHAPTER 1

Up from Pine Level

NOBODY KNOWS EXACTLY where in Tuskegee, Alabama, Rosa McCauley was born on February 4, 1913. The town newspaper reported that the skies were clear and it was unseasonably warm that day, but beyond that, and the fact that she was named after her maternal grandmother, Rose, virtually no reliable documentation exists on the early years of Rosa Louise Parks. It wouldn't matter so much were not some entrepreneurial Tuskegeeans anxious to attract tourists by opening a multicultural human and civil rights center boasting her name, and others, less commerce-minded, eager to post a bronze plaque somewhere in town marking her inclusion in Tuskegee's extraordinary roster of African-American heroes, from Booker T. Washington to George Washington Carver to Ralph Ellison.

A photograph does exist of Rosa Parks's Tuskegee birthplace, but it raises more questions than it answers. The faded photo shows a plywood shanty fronted by six wobbly steps leading up to a porch seemingly on the verge of collapse. A portion of the front picture window has been shattered as though from a rock thrown into the living room, and the picket fence that marks the property is severely splintered. But for a sturdy brick chimney, the edifice would appear no better than the sharecroppers' shacks photographed so hauntingly by Walker Evans in *Let Us Now Praise Famous Men*. But it's another disparity that dominates the picture: Carved into the roof's rough wood is a large star in the style of the *distelfinks* Amish farmers hang on their barns in Pennsylvania's Dutch country. Just as nobody knows where the house was, nobody knows when or why the star was carved on Parks's birthplace—or what, if anything, it signifies. This has not kept some of Alabama's Christian mystics from insisting it was a sign, like the Star of Bethlehem, that God had a special interest in bringing Rosa Parks into the world.

Indeed: Even as a dreamy, mild-mannered young girl, Rosa McCauley had found the black pulpit intoxicating in the openness it accorded preachers to weave the joyous exaltations and heartrending laments that were legacies of the West African culture passed down from generations of slaves to the sharecroppers of 1920s Alabama. "The church, with its musical rhythms and echoes of Africa, thrilled me when I was young," Parks recalled. For a long time Southern whites hadn't wanted blacks to become Christians, preferring to pretend that slaves had no souls. From 1619, when the first human captives landed in Virginia, until 1773 there were no black churches anywhere in America, and the only blacks in white churches were relegated to the galleries. But from the Revolutionary War era onward, African Americans took not only the Bible but organized religious gatherings and rituals as passionately to heart as their ancestors had those of their native African faiths, such as the Yoruba religion, whose adherents memorized thousands of proverbs and allegories. Some Yoruba priests brought over on slave ships could recite a King James Bible's worth of African religious teachings, a practice that lived on in African-American Christianity.

Thus it was that at an early age the inquisitive Rosa Mc-Cauley began memorizing Bible verses, routinely quoting Scripture with Sunday school pride. Naturally demure, she was reserved in church, but just hearing her family and friends shouting "Amen!" and "Hallelujah!" filled Parks with a certitude in her deep Christian faith. "God is everything to me," she explained.

All her life Rosa Parks remained a devoted member of the African Methodist Episcopal (AME) Church, founded in 1816 in Philadelphia by the Bishop Richard Allen, a former slave. From its inception, the AME Church, through its *Freedom's Journal*, petitioned legislatures to end slavery. The Charleston slave rebellion of 1822, led by Denmark Vesey, was, in fact, organized around the AME Church. Congregationalists soon included Frederick Douglass, Harriet Tubman, and Sojourner Truth. "The denomination became known as 'The Freedom Church' during the abolitionist movement," Parks proudly boasts. "It was the spiritual home of many well-known black persons in our history before civil rights." The first AME church in Alabama was established in Mobile fifty years later, as AME churches spread throughout the South after the Civil War; it counted nearly seven thousand congregations with over half a million members when Rosa Mc-Cauley was born in 1913. Hymns played a large part in the AME Sunday service, which spawned the gospel-music genre from the singing and shouting and dancing in ecstatic celebration of Jesus Christ. Although they observed the same Communion rituals as traditional Methodist churches, AME preachers didn't just intone passages from the New Testament; they used impassioned oratory to bring the spirit of the Lord right into their congregations. Early AME bishops often tended toward black nationalism and advocated missionary efforts in Africa. To this day, AME ministers challenge America to live up to its ideals of equality for all.

In her 1994 book *Quiet Strength,* Parks described how her belief in Christ as humanity's savior developed after her baptism in the AME Church at the age of two. "In those days, they sprinkled us with water like the Catholics did," she recalled. With no prodding from her parents, Rosa McCauley was soon performing daily devotions, praying frequently, and going to church as often as possible. "I was never pressed, against my will, to go to church," she wrote. "I always wanted to go." Afflicted by chronic tonsillitis, as a child Rosa often stayed sick in bed for days, unable to swallow without terrible pain. The condition lasted until she was nine and her mother could finally afford to pay for a tonsillectomy in Montgomery. A shy loner with no real friends, Rosa learned to find comfort in Christian hymns such as "Woke Up This Morning with My Mind Stayed on Jesus" and "Oh, Freedom, Let it Ring," which her mother had sung to her as a baby. Faith in God was never the question for Rosa Parks; it was the answer. All her life she disagreed with novelist James Baldwin's strident claim that "to be black in America is to live in a constant stage of rage." The teachings of Jesus Christ had convinced her instead, as they had Martin Luther King, Jr., that a heart filled with love could conquer anything, even bigotry. "I remember finding such comfort and peace while reading the Bible," Parks averred. "Its teaching became a way of life and helped me in dealing with my day-to-day problems." She did, however, augment her nonviolent disposition with a belief that revenge was sometimes necessary. "From my upbringing and the Bible I learned people should stand up for rights," she recalled, "just as the children of Israel stood up to the Pharaoh."

Rosa's father, James McCauley, hailed from Abbeville, Alabama, a farm town ninety-five miles south of Montgomery known for its wood pulp and cotton gins. With his light skin, thick, wavy hair, and broad shoulders, McCauley was sometimes mistaken for a Cherokee or Creek Indian, owing to the fact that one of his grandmothers was a part-Indian slave. A skilled carpenter and stonemason, McCauley built houses all over Alabama's Black Belt region, a 4,300-mile strip of rolling prairie land underlain by a sticky black clay soil ideal for growing cotton. McCauley met Rosa's mother— Leona Edwards, a beautiful, prim-and-proper schoolteacher— in Pine Level, Alabama, a town not far from Abbeville. Blessed with an insatiable desire to learn, Edwards had been schooled in Selma and done undergraduate study organized by the AME chapter at Payne University, though she never earned a degree.

The pastor of Pine Level's Mount Zion AME Church—a close relative of Edwards—married the two twenty-four-year-olds there on April 12, 1912, the same day the *Titanic* left on its ill-fated transatlantic journey. Soon after, the McCauleys moved to Tuskegee and had their first baby, Rosa Louise, who would later recall, "I came along, and I was a sickly child, small for my age. It was probably hard for my mother to take care of me." To make matters more difficult, James McCauley's brother, Robert, came to live with the young family, requiring Leona McCauley to cook and wash and make a home for him, too. "She had to quit teaching until after I was born, and she always talked about how unhappy she was, being an expectant mother and not knowing many people," Rosa Parks would remember. "At that time women who were pregnant didn't get out and move around and socialize like they do now." But Leona Edwards McCauley, determined on betterment for her baby, harbored a bold hope: that just being in Tuskegee, the best place in Alabama for African Americans to educate themselves, would rub off on her daughter. Thus, she taught Rosa that Alabama's segregationist state motto—*Audemus jura nostra defendere* ("We dare defend our rights")—could also be interpreted as a rallying cry for black pride.

When Rosa McCauley was born in 1913, Tuskegee—population three thousand—had already reached its zenith as a citadel of black intellectual life, thanks to Booker T. Washington. Born into slavery in Virginia and raised during Reconstruction, Washington had come to Alabama in 1881 with the express purpose of founding the Tuskegee Normal Industrial Institute. "I find Tuskegee a beautiful little town, with high and healthy location," Washington had described it in a letter on July 14, 1881. "It is a town such as one rarely sees in the South. Its quiet shady streets and tasteful and rich dwellings remind one of a New England village." Indefatigable, optimistic, and frenetic, Washington was a man eminently in sync with the spirit of his time, and he guided Tuskegee's development to phenomenal success. By September 1895, when Washington made his famous speech at the Atlanta Cotton States and International Exposition spelling out his pragmatic philosophy on race relations and higher education for all Americans, Tuskegee already held a prominent place in African-American scholarship, an achievement for which Harvard University had recognized him with an honorary doctorate.

Booker T. Washington's influence was unprecedented for a black American: Even Presidents Theodore Roosevelt and William Howard Taft looked to him for advice on solving race problems and making political appointments of African Americans. Considered the most important black leader since Frederick Douglass, Washington was forever on the move, rarely at rest: He traveled to make speeches and raise funds, his life's mission the continual improvement of the Tuskegee Institute. Even his critics concede that he was a genius at navigating the racial divide, and when he died on the morning of November 14, 1915, all of Tuskegee mourned.

To understand the African-American condition when Rosa McCauley was born, it is illuminating to read the February 1913 edition of the NAACP's monthly journal, *The Crisis*, which editor W. E. B. Du Bois dubbed the "record of the darker races." Under the rubric "The Burden," *The Crisis* published a harrowing tally of the names and hometowns of blacks lynched or burned for supposed crimes—sixty-three documented cases in 1912 alone, in cities from Muldrow, Oklahoma, to Greenville, South Carolina. That same February, Booker T. Washington wrote a letter from Tuskegee to William Malone Baskerville, news editor for the southern district of the Associated Press, condemning American cities like Atlanta where "a man could be punished for beating a horse or killing birds" but it was impossible "to prevent a mob from burning and torturing a human being."

Rosa McCauley lived in Tuskegee only until the age of two—too young to remember hearing Booker T. Washington hold forth at Tompkins Hall on the virtues of personal hygiene or to attend a religious service at the Pavilion, a large tentlike structure on campus. But her mother took the philosophy of the Tuskegee Institute with them and schooled her daughter in it. "My mother was very much impressed by Booker T. Washington," Rosa Parks recalled. "She admired his ability." The McCauley household embraced Washington's notion that high moral character and absolute cleanliness were "civilizing agents" that would help blacks excel in America. "I never see a filthy yard that I do not want to clean it . . . or a button off one's clothes, or a grease-spot on them or on a floor, that I do not want to call attention to it," Washington had said, and so the McCauleys did.

Along with the Bible, Washington's 1901 autobiography, *Up from Slavery*, was a fixture in the McCauley house, and years later Rosa Parks told an interviewer that she shared the author's belief in the power of hard work and rigorous thrift. Like many African Americans of the time, Leona McCauley devoured and embraced Washington's "self-help" books, particularly chapters such as "Working with the Hands," "Putting the Most into Life," and "Sowing and Reaping." Echoing Tuskegee's great agricultural botanist and chemist George Washington Carver, her mother also taught young Rosa that there was a use for everything on earth. "I indulge in very little lip service," Carver had declared, "but ask the Great Creator silently, daily, and often many times a day to permit me to speak to Him through the three great kingdoms of the world which He created—the animal, mineral, and vegetable kingdoms—to understand their relations to each other, and our relations to them and to the Great God who made all of us." On the same principle, little Rosa McCauley learned to make baskets out of pine needles and corn husks.

As she grew older, she memorized Paul Lawrence Dunbar's poem "The Tuskegee Song."

In his 1971 collection *South to a Very Old Place*, essayist Albert Murray tells of arriving in Tuskegee, halfway between Columbus, Georgia, and Montgomery, Alabama, by bus on U.S. Route 80 East, gazing out the window upon the swamp-lands and pecan orchards dotting the gently rolling hills under a pale blue central Alabama sky blowing a melancholy back-to-school breeze. Groves of towering pines grew out of the sandy red soil, and hungry hawks circled overhead searching for field mice and moles. A daydreaming Murray would "let the seat back" and enjoy the "heavy-duty-rubber-on-open-country-asphalt road hum." Small Protestant churches often posed Welcome signs in front with sayings like: "If you can say ABC, then Jesus says come unto me: A = admit B = believe C = commit." But despite the dazzling landscape and Christian come-ons, no matter how hard they tried, Rosa McCauley's parents found little joy in their dirt-road poverty and the strains it put on their marriage.

Like many Alabama families, the McCauleys had indirectly fallen victim to a plague, not of locusts but of weevils. Indigenous to Mexico and never seen in the United States until it crossed the Rio Grande in 1893, the boll weevil—a small, long-beaked gray beetle that lays its eggs only in the immature bolls of cotton plants, which its larvae then destroy—slowly crawled east and first appeared in Alabama in 1918, devastating the state's cotton plantations and ending its prosperity. Although George Washington Carver had been trying to teach African-American farmers the importance of crop diversification—he would win international fame in the 1920s for his experiments with sweet potatoes, cowpeas, and peanuts—few had listened; cotton was simply more lucrative. Thus, the initial infestation sent the many communities entirely dependent on cotton into boll-weevil panics and unleashed a wave of despair through the Deep South. "As the plantation deteriorates, the big houses go without paint, the roof leaks, the porches tumble down, one field and then another is abandoned to brambles and gullies," sociologist Arthur F. Raper wrote of the sudden collapse of the Black Belt economy. Medical care in Alabama's largely African-American cotton communities fell to near-nonexistent levels, and malnutrition spread as salt pork, hominy grits, cornbread, and molasses became the staples and fresh milk, fruits, and vegetables almost impossible to come by. Even nonfarm families like the McCauleys suffered the region's hard times—and slowly adapted as its agriculture shifted from planting cotton to hay cropping, dairying, and raising livestock. As William Faulkner once suggested, a heroic capacity of African Americans is that "they endure"—which the roving McCauleys believed they could do more success-fully in Abbeville, where family members were willing to support them for a while.

So they moved in with James McCauley's parents and large extended family, four children sharing a bedroom with a dirt floor. Leona McCauley found it difficult to raise Rosa in such overcrowded conditions, especially since she didn't get along with her in-laws. With her husband, James, inattentive to his family's needs even when his itinerant vocation didn't keep him away for months at a time, Leona McCauley left Abbeville with Rosa still in diapers and moved back in with her own family in Pine Level. After that, James McCauley virtually disappeared from his daughter's life, preferring to wander the countryside with his hammer, saw, and adulterous eyes. "He left Pine Level to find work, and I did not see him again until I was five years old and my brother was three," Rosa Parks remembered sadly. "He stayed several days and left again. I did not see my father any more until I was an adult and married."

Pine Level was a forgettable flyspeck of a town, like thousands of others scattered across the South, a place where poor blacks toiled for poor whites under often grueling circumstances. The rhythms of the King James Bible echoed in every household, white and black, and Rosa McCauley essentially grew up in the white-framed Mount Zion AME Church on old Route 231, where her uncle was the preacher. She was an equable girl, content with her own company, but just as happy scooping crawfish with the other neighborhood children to bring home for a boiling with fresh corn. Although they were poor, there was ample food, and on special occasions the McCauleys would indulge in fried ham with red-eye gravy, catfish fillets, or braised rabbit, accompanied by turnip greens, creamed peas, and pearl onions. And for dessert it was always sweet potato pie.

As a fatherless child in Pine Level, Rosa counted on her mother for love and comfort. Often, however, Leona McCauley was elsewhere in the county teaching at far-flung black church schools, so Rosa was raised in part by her grandparents. From them Rosa Parks heard about Union general William Tecumseh Sherman's incendiary March to the Sea through Georgia; about President Abraham Lincoln's Emancipation Proclamation, freeing them from white slave owner John Edwards's whip; about how during Reconstruction they purchased twelve acres of plantation land in hopes of restarting their lives as free Americans. And she also learned that one of her maternal great-grandfathers, James Percival—an indentured servant of Pine Level's Wright family—was a white Scotch-Irishman who had emigrated to Charleston, South Carolina.

Early on Rosa McCauley learned she was not a full Negro but of mixed blood, a mulatto. In fact, several of her family members were often mistaken for white; her younger brother, Sylvester, was so light-skinned that his slanted eyes inspired people to call him "Chink," thinking he was Asian. Parks also recalled, "My grandfather was very light-complected, with straight hair, and sometimes people took him for white." What's more, "He took every bit of advantage of being white-looking. He was always doing or saying something that would embarrass or agitate white people." She particularly remembered the way he would shake hands with whites in defiance of the time's taboo on interracial handshaking, and introduce himself as "Edwards" despite the Jim Crow etiquette that black men introduce themselves only by their first names and always address whites as "Mister" or "Miss." Watching her grandfather flout society's race rules gave Rosa McCauley her first taste of overt civil disobedience against discrimination. "My grandfather had a somewhat belligerent attitude toward whites in general," Parks explained later. "And he liked to laugh at whites behind their backs."

When Rosa McCauley was ten, she got an unexpected lesson in the extent to which skin color dominated the culture of the American South. Her grandfather had been an early supporter of the Jamaican-born Marcus Garvey, whose Harlem-based Universal Negro Improvement Association, founded in 1916, called for blacks to emigrate back to Africa. Influenced by Washington's *Up from Slavery*, Garvey advocated a "new world of *Black* men, not peons, serfs, dogs, and slaves," a righteous vision young Rosa's maternal grandfather cheered. That changed in 1923, when a delegation of Garveyites came to Montgomery County and held a public forum. "My grandfather, who had been a slave when he was a little boy, looked exactly like the white people did," Parks recalled. "He did attend the meeting, but he was rejected because of his white appearance. That ended our talking about our going back to Africa."

Instead, Rosa's grandfather Edwards concentrated on protecting his family from white predators. Lynchings of blacks had become commonplace thanks to the resurgence of the Ku Klux Klan, a southern terrorist movement first spawned after the Civil War and reorganized nearly half a century later on Thanksgiving Day 1915 at Georgia's Stone Mountain. There, under an American flag and the glow of a burning cross, sixteen racists, inspired by their misinterpretation of D. W. Griffith's new film *Birth of a Nation*, pledged themselves to the cause of "white supremacy." They proved their dedication by performing ridiculous cultish rituals while vowing all too sincerely to rid American society of blacks, Jews, Catholics, and other "undesirables."

The rebirth of the Klan was in part a noxious outgrowth of World War I. Emboldened by the racial harmony they had witnessed in Europe, African-American soldiers returning from the trenches of Belgium and France had begun to demand equal rights at home. At the same time, many rural southern blacks, fleeing from the boll weevil's decimation of the cotton industry, headed north in the Great Migration to establish new lives in urban centers, fueling a new wave of antiblack resentment among white workers anxious for the same scarce jobs. By mid-1919, race riots were so prevalent and bloody that writer James Weldon Johnson dubbed the period America's "Red Summer."

In this poisonous atmosphere the Ku Klux Klan thrived; eighty-five thousand men joined the order between June 1920 and October 1921 alone. "By the time I was six, I was old enough to realize that we were not actually free," Rosa Parks would remember. "The Ku Klux Klan was riding through the black community, burning churches, beating up people, killing people." Between 1885 and 1918 some 250 blacks were lynched in Alabama, most of the later murders overseen by the Klan.

Historians writing about the Klan's rise through the 1920s often note that only 16 percent of the group's members lived in the South. Indeed, there were more Klansmen in New Jersey than Alabama; Klan membership in Indianapolis was nearly double that in South Carolina and Mississippi combined. But what these statistics ignore is the "terror index," a measure of the Ku Klux Klan's regional strength by its degree of violence. By any measure, Alabama's Black Belt counties would have ranked near the very top of the terror barometer. What's more, by 1927 Alabama's most powerful politicians— Democratic U.S. senator (and later liberal U.S. Supreme Court justice) Hugo Black, Governor David Bibbs Graves, and State Attorney General Charles McCall—were all proud members of the KKK.

Rosa Parks remembered how her grandfather responded to the threat by keeping a double-barreled shotgun close at hand at all times, loaded and ready for the first hooded bigot who trespassed onto his property. "And I remember we talked about how just in case the Klansmen broke into our house, we should go to bed with our clothes on so we would be ready to run if we had to," she added. "I can remember my grandfather saying, 'I don't know how long I would last if they came breaking in here, but I'm getting the first one who comes through the door.'"

It is heartbreaking to think of any child having youth's innocence shattered by the prospect of torture and death at the hands of jackbooted Nazis or hooded Klansmen. Yet it was from that prospect that young Rosa McCauley learned it wasn't enough to just "turn a cheek" in Christian submission when one's very life was at stake. So every night, as her grandfather slept in a rocking chair by the fireplace with his shotgun in his lap, Rosa curled up on the floor beside him, ready to spring to the defense of her home. "I remember thinking that whatever happened, I wanted to see it," Parks explained decades later. "I wanted to see him shoot that gun."

Fortunately, although the Klan used to parade up and down the road in front of the Edwards's house, they never attacked, and unlike Malcolm X in his autobiography, Parks never felt the need to fictionalize a direct showdown with them. But from a very early age she felt the violence of white supremacism, the institutionalized racism that made it life-threatening to break the South's Jim Crow laws. Well before adolescence she learned what it felt like to be treated as a beast of burden from Moses Hudson, the wealthiest planter in Pine Level, who used to hire barefoot black children to pick and chop cotton for fifty cents a day. "We had a saying," Parks recalled, "that we worked from can to can't, which means working from when you can see [sunup] to when you can't [sundown]. I never will forget how the sun just burned into me. The hot sand burned our feet whether or not we had our old work shoes on." When the ensuing blisters made it too painful to stand, whole teams of child workers would be forced to pick their ways down the cotton rows on their knees. "There were only two sets of good shoes in the field: on Mr. Freeman, the white overseer," Parks recalled, "and on the horse he rode through the field." If a child got blood on the white cotton, Moses Hudson had the offender whipped.

Despite all she endured at the hands of some whites, Rosa McCauley Parks never fell to judging the whole race by the behavior of a few of its members, however appalling. In later years she would tell of the kindness of an old woman in Pine Level who used to take her bass fishing with crawfish tails as bait—an old white woman who treated her grandparents as equals. Even as a girl she appreciated that it was northern white industrialists with names like Carnegie, Huntington, and Rockefeller who were responsible for financing many of the Tuskegee Institute's exquisite redbrick buildings. And she never forgot the white World War I Yankee doughboy who came to town and patted her kindly on the head in passing, an unheard-of gesture in the South. Her Christian faith only made her feel sorry for the white tormentors who called her "nigger" or threw rocks at her as she walked to school. Reading Psalms 23 and 27 early on had given Rosa Mc-Cauley the strength to love her enemy.

Under her grandfather's fierce influence, she grew up believing what Marcus Garvey preached: that Negroes were the "direct descendants of the greatest and proudest race who ever peopled the earth." Thus unencumbered by any sense of inferiority despite the nightly Klan watch, the little girl could delight in the discoveries and innocent adventures of childhood. In her autobiography, *My Story*, Parks tells happily of the grammar lessons she gobbled up at the little frame schoolhouse in Pine Level, next to Mount Zion AME Church; of her infatuation with Mother Goose nursery rhymes, particularly "Little Red Riding Hood"; of playing "ring games" like "Little Sally Walker Sitting in the Saucer" and "Rise, Sally, Rise"; of fussing over her little brother, Sylvester, like a mother hen; of selling eggs and chickens to neighbors for extra pocket money; and of exploring the dense pine thicket along creeks and ponds, careful to avoid coral snakes, water moccasins, and copperheads. Hide-and-seek in the nearby narrow skirts of rich woodland was her favorite game, except come May, when the wildflowers exploded in colors across the lush meadows and made running through them her delight.

It intoxicated little Rosa to survey the countryside and imagine Alabama before the days of white settlement, when tremendous herds of bison and elk had thundered onto the prairies to graze; only the white-tailed deer had managed to survive in any significant numbers. Further intimations of mortality came from the weathered graves dating back to the Civil War that stood crooked in the churchyard, where old-timers strolled speaking of Grant's liberation of Vicksburg as if it were yesterday. But when the white boys taunted her as "nigger," Rosa McCauley ever held her own and refused to sulk away ashamed. For it had been "passed down almost in our genes," she would explain, that a proud African American simply could not accept "bad treatment from anybody."

CHAPTER 2

Coming of Age in Montgomery

SOME THREE-QUARTERS of a century after the event, Rosa Parks still vividly recalled the time a boy on roller skates tried to slam her off a sidewalk as she walked through his all-white neighborhood. "I turned around and pushed him," she remembered. "A white woman was standing not too far from us. She turned out to be his mother, because she said she could put me so far in jail that I never would get out again for pushing her child. So I told her that he had pushed me and that I didn't want to be pushed, seeing that I wasn't bothering him at all." This and many other stories like it show that the outwardly demure Parks had a defiant streak from the start. "Nobody ever bossed Rosa around and got away with it," one childhood friend put it. Parks herself attributed her independence to the teachings of her grandfather and of a white teacher from Melrose, Massachusetts, who ran the school that first introduced Rosa Parks to the wider world.

When Rosa McCauley turned eleven in 1924, her mother enrolled her at the Montgomery Industrial School for Girls, a uniquely progressive institution that had been founded the year after the Civil War ended. It stood at 601–603 South Union Street in the Centennial Hill neighborhood, Montgomery's center of black intellectual life. Better known as Miss White's Industrial School for Girls, both its cofounders, Alice L. White and Margaret Beard, and all of its teachers were white, while the student body of 250 to 300 girls was entirely black. "They didn't talk to us about color," remembered Emma Dungree Allen, who attended Miss White's with Parks in the 1920s. "The biggest thing they emphasized was [that] cleanliness was next to godliness."

Miss White ran her school with a focus on the domestic sciences of cooking, sewing, and housekeeping, a pragmatic vocational approach inspired in part by Booker T. Washington, who heartily approved of the school's educational strategy. "I have kept up with the work that Misses White and Beard are doing in the Montgomery, Alabama, Industrial School, and have no hesitation in saying that they are doing good, practical work in that city," he wrote in a fund-raising letter for the school. "Especially this is true in the way they connect the work done in the schoolroom with [that in] the homes of their pupils. I find that they keep out of debt and spend the money that is given them economically and wisely."

Today, driving through the forty blocks surrounding the intersection of High and Jackson Streets, past the endless condemned buildings and squalor, it is hard to imagine that the area was once the city's most prestigious African-American district. But Centennial Hill boasts three houses listed in the National Register and thirteen more designated historic locally. By the time Woodrow Wilson was president, Centennial Hill ranked alongside Atlanta's Sweet Auburn area as one of the South's showplace black business districts. But what made Centennial Hill special—what drew future civil rights leaders, such as Ralph Abernathy and Martin

Luther King, Jr., to make the neighborhood their home—was its abundance of progressive educational institutions for blacks: the Swayne School, Centennial Hill High School, the State Normal School for Colored Students (now Alabama State University), and Miss White's Industrial School for Girls, which together trained the generation of civil rights activists who would emerge in the 1950s.

To a country girl like Rosa McCauley, Montgomery in the Roaring Twenties was the big city indeed, a Technicolor Oz topped off by the imposing, ninety-seven-foot-high white dome of the Capitol on Goat Hill. Model Ts choked the streets; antebellum Greek Revival mansions glittered with the affluence of King Cotton; stores sold a vast array of wonderful things, one even on Sundays; the Louisville & Nashville railroad came roaring into Union Station from the hinterland; Alabama River boats dropped off their cargoes of pine timber and baled cotton at the bustling wharf; radio stations blared everything from Beethoven to Ma Rainey's soulful Georgia blues, and a twelve-thousand-seat football stadium—the Cramton Bowl, built in 1922 on Madison Avenue—made it clear that Montgomery sure was no hick town. Indeed, the city considered itself as a forward-looking crossroads where planters in shiny Levi Strauss overalls and mud-caked work boots could mingle at harvest time with well-heeled executives from Birmingham and seafaring merchants from Mobile Bay under the languid ceiling fans in the lobby of the Court Square Exchange Hotel. By the World War II years, an explosion of textile and garment factories, cotton-processing plants, and fertilizer warehouses had revamped Montgomery into a lively, modern service center for farmers and businessmen throughout the region. Yet for all its advancement, Alabama's capital city clung to Jim Crow as fiercely as any small town in the rural Deep South.

The term "Jim Crow" is believed to have come from a minstrel show first staged in 1828 by white entertainer Thomas "Daddy" Rice, who performed a song-and-dance routine called "Jump Jim Crow" in burned-cork blackface and hobo rags. Later in the nineteenth century, Jim Crow took on a more sinister meaning: the official system of racial segregation that spread across the South after the Civil War. Beginning around 1875, blacks and whites were legally separated on streetcars, trains, steamboats, and every other mode of transportation as well as at schools, hospitals, restaurants, hotels, barbershops, theaters, even drinking fountains. Segregation laws slapped "white" and "colored" signs on virtually every facility, signs that served, in the words of historian C. V. Woodward, as "the public symbols and constant reminders" of blacks' supposed juniority.

In 1920s Montgomery, the Jim Crow trolley that ran downtown demanded that blacks enter from the rear and stay there. The public bus that ran between Montgomery and Tuskegee refused to let "colored people" inside. African Americans had to sit on top with the luggage, no matter the weather. "We were tenth-class citizens in the eyes of our country," recalled former Joint Chiefs of Staff chairman and U.S. Army general Colin Powell. "The flame under the melting pot was unlit when it came to African Americans."

This is not to say that southern blacks took the callous discrimination in stride. Ever since the U.S. Supreme Court's 1896 decision in *Plessy v. Ferguson* authorizing "separate but equal" public conveyances, outraged African Americans throughout the South had been organizing pro-integration protest rallies. In the first decade of the twentieth century, blacks in twenty-seven Deep South cities boycotted segregated streetcars. Montgomery, which boasted the first electric trolley system in the country, was confronted with a massive boycott in August 1900 when African-American ministers urged their congregations to walk rather than ride, in a show of solidarity against the city's unfairness to its paying passengers. "Montgomery is experiencing the most unique boycott in history," the *Atlanta Constitution* reported on September 20 of that year. Five successive weeks of blacks' refusal to ride the streetcars had cost the trolley operator 25 percent of its business. Eventually the company capitulated and ended streetcar segregation in the city, but the victory was short-lived; by the 1920s, in part because of the Klan's reemergence, Jim Crow returned to the Montgomery trolley lines. Nevertheless, the streetcar boycott of 1900—a largely forgotten episode in civil rights history—was an important precursor to the 1955 Montgomery bus boycott that would bring Rosa Parks international recognition. "I had heard stories about the 1900 boycott," Parks recalled. "I thought about it sometimes when the segregated trolley passed by. It saddened me to think how we had taken one foot forward and two steps back."

What fueled her historic refusal was the character Rosa McCauley forged from her own experiences combined with what she learned at home and school. Her maternal grandfather, of course, had taught her to stand up for herself, but her mother had imbued her with the more pragmatic and patient philosophy of Booker T. Washington. In 1954, four decades after his death, his more radical successor as America's leading black intellectual, National Association for the Advancement of Colored People (NAACP) founder W. E. B. Du Bois, still complained that "Washington was a politician. He was a man who believed that we should get what we could get." But even Du Bois had to admit his precursor knew the "heart of the South from birth and training." The folksy Washington's so-called and much-maligned accommodationist approach was only what he considered a necessary stepping-stone on the path to true equal rights attained without bloodshed by or against blacks.

To Booker T. Washington, vocational education was a pragmatic way for African Americans to achieve economic power, a central theme today of the Reverend Jesse Jackson's Operation PUSH. Speaking in the early 1900s, Washington—unlike Du Bois later—was wise to reject Karl Marx's dangerous notion that political revolution was a necessary prerequisite to economic empowerment. To have espoused such a belief at the turn of the century would have led to the wholesale slaughter of southern blacks.

Yet Washington worked tirelessly behind the scenes to overturn the *Plessy v. Ferguson* decision and to undermine and then eradicate dozens of Jim Crow's other legalized affronts to blacks. Anyone who doubts Washington's commitment to ending racial discrimination should read his November 1912 polemic in *Century* magazine, "Is the Negro Having a Fair Chance?" As editor and critic William Dean Howells summed it up, at the time, Washington's nonconfrontational approach to the civil rights problem was "the only way for his race."

All in all, Washington was addressing racial inequities in the context of the socioeconomic realities of an agrarian South in which 75 percent of all African Americans lived early in the twentieth century. What the next generation of northern activists from Boston and New York failed to appreciate was just how backward things were even in the biggest southern cities. Up until 1946, Montgomery, for example, had no public high schools for the nearly fifty thousand African Americans who called the city home. Thus, it makes perfect sense that Washington supported institutions such as Miss White's Montgomery Industrial School for Girls, the only place an eager adolescent like Rosa McCauley could get a quality education in the Alabama state capital back then.

In addition to operating on Booker T. Washington's no-nonsense principles for getting ahead as an African American, Miss White's School was a bastion of strict Christian morality where the New Testament was read daily and prayer formed an integral part of every class. The devout Rosa McCauley excelled in this regard, according to Johnnie Mae Carr, a friend since they entered the fifth grade together. Years later Carr, the first woman to join the Montgomery NAACP and one who would play a pivotal role in the Montgomery bus boycott, recalled how "very quiet" Rosa was at school, always sitting up straight, always obeying Miss White, and "staying out of trouble." Their teachers forbade dancing, for instance, but one of the few girls who observed the injunction was Rosa McCauley. "She refused to dance outside the school because she believed it was immoral," Carr related. "She was a straight Christian arrow."

The ratification of the Nineteenth Amendment in 1920 had given women the right to vote and triggered a Jazz Age wave of sexual liberation, but its effects were scarcely felt in Alabama, and were forbidden at the Montgomery Industrial

School for Girls. The quintessence of "flaming youth" during this era may have been Montgomery's own Zelda Sayre, who in 1920 married F. Scott Fitzgerald, but Rosa Parks never learned any of the new jazz dances like the Shimmy, the Bunny Hug, or the Buzzard Lope. Blues singer Bessie Smith may have been suggesting new options to modern women throughout Harlem in racy songs like "I'm Wild About That Thing" and "Nobody in Town Can Bake a Sweet Jelly Roll Like Mine," but at Miss White's School "Amazing Grace" remained the standard. A believer in temperance, White saw to it that her girls did not sully their virtue with such vanities as Madame C. J. Walker's hair straightener, red lipstick, or silver hoop earrings, as modeled on the cover of *Opportunity*, the Urban League's journal of Negro life. "Even going to the movies was considered sinful," Carr remembered. "Miss White would punish us if we became undisciplined or in any way undermined our self-esteem."

Miss Alice L. White—disciplinarian, teetotaler, and loving teacher—loomed large in the memories of her pupils. Both Rosa Parks and Johnnie Mae Carr looked back on her school, and especially its strict standards, as guideposts in their growth as civil rights activists. "What I learned best at Miss White's School was that I was a person with dignity and self-respect and I should not set my sights lower than anybody just because I was black," Parks explained. "We were taught to be ambitious and to believe that we could do what we wanted in life."

Unfortunately for its students at the time, as well as the girls who would have benefited from it in the future, Miss White's school was forced to close after Rosa McCauley finished the eighth grade in 1928. Long a thorn in the side of white Montgomery, which harbored a general hostility toward "northern abolitionist types," Miss White and her teachers had always been socially ostracized, accused of teaching "racial equality" and called "Yankee nigger lovers." Their school was even burned to the ground earlier in the century. As the Klan's power grew, the Montgomery Industrial School for Girls had become a prime target. Miss White had grown old, blind, and infirm but nevertheless was essentially run out of town. She headed back home to Melrose, Massachusetts, with no idea just how profound an impression her teachings had made on scores of girls who would spark the modern civil rights movement. A long letter Miss White wrote to Rosa McCauley shortly before she died remained one of Parks's cherished keepsakes and a reminder that not all white people were racists.

After the school closed, fifteen-year-old Rosa McCauley stayed on in Centennial Hill to attend the ninth grade at Booker T. Washington Junior High, formerly the Swayne School, and tenth and eleventh grades at the laboratory school at Alabama State Teachers College for Negroes. She wanted to become a professional educator like her mother but was forced to abandon her studies after her grandmother fell ill and needed Rosa to care for her back home in Pine Level. When her grandmother died a month later, Rosa, then sixteen, returned to Montgomery to take her first real job: making men's blue denim work shirts at a textile factory. It wasn't long before she had to quit and drop out again, this time to care for her mother, who suffered from migraine headaches and painfully swollen feet. "I was not happy about dropping out of school either time," Parks averred, "but it was my responsibility to help with my grandmother and later to take care of my mother. I did not complain; it was just something that had to be done."

Art critics have generally failed to note that Walker Evans chose to photograph only white tenant farmers in Hale County, Alabama, because, as his collaborator James Agee put it, poor Negroes were "of the sootiest black which no light can make shine." It is therefore fortunate that Swiss photojournalist Annemarie Schwarzenbach toured the South in 1937 documenting both Montgomery's black business district, known as Monroe Avenue, and the rural sharecroppers throughout the Black Belt region. Her haunting Alabama photographs of African Americans during the Great Depression offer a marvelous visual record of the world in which Rosa Parks grew up: a poor woman hanging laundry on a breezy afternoon, ramshackle cabins with barefoot boys studying the horizon, an old-timer parking his mule-drawn carriage among the automobiles of downtown Montgomery, bales of oozing cotton ready to be shipped, the Southern Hotel balcony looking as if it were conceived in the Vieux Carre, hot fieldhands taking a Coca-Cola break. As a realist photographer, Schwarzenbach captured something no Works Progress Administration guide or newspaper article did: The blacks in her portraits stare forlornly into the distance, waiting for something to happen as they gaze at the camera with expressions of mute despair.

Rosa McCauley spent the rest of her teenage years acting the stoic Christian, firm in the belief that complaining about one's lot only made it harder to endure. She was a devoted member of St. Paul AME Church, located on Hardaway Street in the BelAir subdivision, the oldest black neighborhood in Montgomery. The church was the center of Rosa's life, bringing her spiritual joy, while her days essentially re-volved around hard work—cleaning white people's houses and taking in sewing on the side. Occasionally she sold fruit on the street or at fairs. That pattern—and her political com-placency—ended when she fell in love with Raymond Parks.

Born on February 12, 1903, in the village of Wedowee, northeast of Montgomery, Raymond Parks knew hard times early. His carpenter father, David Parks, had fallen off a roof and died when he was an infant. His mother, Geri Culbert-son Parks, taught him to read and write but died when Ray-mond was in his teens. Raised among white people—and, like Rosa McCauley's grandfather, so light-skinned that he was often mistaken for Caucasian—Raymond Parks worked as a sexton at a church in Roanoke County, Alabama, before heading to Tuskegee when he was twenty-eight years old. There he learned how to cut hair before moving on again, and he was working at O. L. Campbell's barbershop in down-town Montgomery when he first laid eyes on the eighteen-year-old Rosa McCauley.

A mutual friend had introduced them, but Rosa said she was uninterested in Raymond's advances, in part because she had "an aversion" to light-skinned blacks. But after weeks of avoiding him, she finally gave in and agreed to a Sunday ride in his shiny red Nash. "I was very impressed by the fact that he didn't seem to have that meek attitude—what we called an 'Uncle Tom' attitude—toward white people," Rosa Parks remembered. "I thought he was a very nice man, an interest-ing man who talked very intelligently. He could talk for hours at a time about all the things he had lived through."

Raymond Parks had been among the charter members of the Montgomery chapter of the NAACP. Well respected in the black community, he not only read *The Crisis* but saw to it that other influential Negro newspapers, such as the *Pittsburgh Courier*, *Amsterdam News*, and *Chicago Defender*, were on hand in his barbershop. Parks greatly admired the poetry of Langston Hughes for its embrace of elements of the African-American vernacular and liked to read aloud from James Weldon Johnson's *God's Trombones: Seven Negro Sermons in Verse*. But when Rosa McCauley met him in 1931, Parks had an all-consuming obsession: the gross injustice being perpetrated by Alabama's criminal justice system upon the so-called Scottsboro Boys. "It gnawed at him to see those innocent kids were framed," she recalled. "He'd say, 'I'll never sleep well until they're free.'"

More than any other civil rights matter of the depression era, the Scottsboro case epitomized the state of race relations in the United States. It began on the afternoon of March 25, 1931, when a Southern Railway freight train bound for Memphis pulled into the yard at Paint Rock, near Scottsboro, Alabama. There armed sheriffs' deputies arrested nine African-American youths, charging them with assaulting a few white boxcar drifters and kicking them off the train. Two white women who had been working as prostitutes also were removed from the train, after which they accused the black men of rape. A wrathful mob formed, and only the efforts of the Jackson County sheriff saved the youths from lynching. A circus trial was arranged, and eight of the boys were convicted of rape by an all-white jury in Scottsboro and given the death penalty; the ninth, just twelve years old, was spared by a hung jury.

The harshness of the teenagers' sentences mobilized public opinion, and in 1932 the U.S. Supreme Court overturned the convictions on the grounds that the accused had not been granted adequate legal counsel. Instantly, the state of Alabama inaugurated a second prosecution of the Scottsboro Boys; at that trial, in 1933, defense attorney Samuel Liebowitz, hired by the Communist-sponsored International Labor Defense, argued their case. The local prosecutor, playing to yet another all-white jury, responded that "Alabama justice cannot be bought and sold with Jew money from New York." But medical doctors determined that the two prostitutes, Ruby Bates and Victoria Price, had lied about having been forced to have sex on the train. For the next half decade lawyers in both the state and federal courts plea-bargained the case. A compromise deal was struck by the youths' defense attorneys in 1937 by which four of the nine defendants were freed and the others condemned to lengthy prison sentences. "The whole Scottsboro ordeal was a travesty of justice," Parks pronounced years later, still bitter. "It's a monument to America at its worst."

When the *Montgomery Advertiser* matter-of-factly labeled the Scottsboro Boys rapists and the local police took to arresting blacks on scant evidence of being Communists, Raymond Parks secretly began a legal defense fund to help the teenagers pay their lawyers to keep them out of the electric chair. From 1931 through 1933, Raymond Parks took part in bimonthly meetings as a member of the National Committee to Defend the Scottsboro Boys—an extremely risky business indeed. "I was proud of Parks for working on behalf of the Scottsboro Boys," Rosa Parks would declare. "I also admired his courage. He could have been beaten or killed for what he was doing." Raymond refused to let her attend any of the meetings, telling her she couldn't run fast enough to escape in the event the police raided the gathering.

Equally bold in matters of the heart, Raymond Parks asked Rosa McCauley to marry him on their second date, and in December 1932, in the midst of the Great Depression, they were wed in Pine Level. With no money for a honeymoon, the couple moved to a rooming house on South Jackson Street in Centennial Hill, not far from Alabama State University. The secret Scottsboro meetings continued, only now in the newlyweds' front room. "There was a little table about the size of a card table that they were sitting around," Rosa Parks remembered of the first one. "The table was covered with guns." While the men strategized, she sat on the back porch with her face buried in her lap. "I didn't move throughout the whole meeting," she recalled. "I was very, very depressed about the fact that black men could not hold a meeting without fear of bodily injury or death."

The civil rights heroism of Raymond Parks has been obscured by his reluctance for his wife to become the symbol of the Montgomery bus boycott and as such a prime target for white violence. But there is no doubt that her husband helped to radicalize Rosa Parks during the Great Depression years, discussing with her all the newest NAACP strategies for helping blacks win the right to vote and gain entry to local hospitals. These were tough times for African Americans in Alabama: they were excluded from juries, hired only for menial jobs, prohibited from enrolling in universities, and denied access to public libraries and parks. To help pull themselves out of these dire straits, Raymond Parks encouraged his young wife to go back to school for her high school diploma, which she earned in 1933. "At that time only a small percentage of black people in Montgomery were high school graduates," Rosa Parks related. "In 1940, seven years after I got my diploma, only seven out of every hundred had as much as a high school diploma."

Although her degree helped build her self-confidence, it did not help her find meaningful employment. Desperate to supplement her husband's barbershop income, Rosa Parks became a nurse's assistant at St. Margaret's Hospital and sewed clothes for white clients on the side. Apart from fading into disrepair, Montgomery had changed little since the Civil War; in fact, Montgomery suffered far less than Alabama's rural countryside during the Great Depression, thanks to the civil-service jobs the state capital had to offer as well as the continuing opportunities at Maxwell Field, an Army Air Corps base two miles outside the city.

In 1941, Rosa Parks got a job at Maxwell Field, established as a flight school by the Wright Brothers themselves, shortly after the base launched an advanced flying program. During World War II, Maxwell Field looked like a clear-cut desert airstrip, with hangars and offices built in prefabricated rows like some precursor to Levittown. The base facilities were, at least in principle, fully integrated—President Franklin D. Roosevelt, whom Parks greatly admired, had forbidden racial segregation in public places and on public conveyances at U.S. military bases. "I could ride on an integrated trolley on the base"—she grimaced—"but when I left the base, I had to ride home on a segregated bus." This disparity annoyed her to no end. Maxwell Field was nearly as integrated as if it were above the Mason-Dixon line, but as soon as she stepped outside its gates, she was relegated to second-class status. Riding home on the segregated city bus became "a humiliation" to her, and one that she grew determined to end. Often overlooked by civil rights historians, her experience with integration at Maxwell was a catalyst of her decision to join the NAACP and fight for the right to vote. It was, in fact, a U.S. military base that showed Rosa Parks, who had never left Alabama, how fair American society could be. "You might just say Maxwell opened my eyes up," Parks believed. "It was an alternative reality to the ugly racial policies of Jim Crow."

CHAPTER 3

A Stirring Passion for Equality

ROSA PARKS DESPERATELY WANTED to vote for Franklin D. Roosevelt in the 1940 presidential election; she admired the president and hoped he would serve an unprecedented third term in the White House. She was particularly enamored of First Lady Eleanor Roosevelt, who had demonstrated her courage by standing up for the African-American singer Marian Anderson in 1939, when she was barred from singing at Washington, D.C.'s Constitution Hall. The first lady made the gallant dramatic gesture of resigning from the Daughters of the American Revolution, which owned the hall, and with the support of Interior Secretary Harold Ickes, arranged for Anderson to sing instead at the Lincoln Memorial on Easter Sunday before a crowd of seventy-five thousand. "In Mrs. Roosevelt you had a white person who truly believed in integration," Parks would later tell a radio interviewer. "She was a caring liberal, a humanitarian—the real thing, and she let Marian Anderson sing."

But even by 1941, when she was working as a secretary in a vestibule at Maxwell Air Force Base, Parks was still denied the ballot box because of her skin color. Officially—compliments of the Reconstruction Act of 1867—African Americans in the South had the right to vote. This had been made explicit in February 1869, when the U.S. Congress passed the Fifteenth Amendment to the Constitution, which the states ratified on February 8, 1870, stating that the right to vote could not be denied "by the United States or by any State on account of race, color, or previous condition of servitude"—although it could still be denied on account of gender. Had the Fifteenth Amendment been enforced, Rosa Parks would have had no trouble voting for the Roosevelts or anyone else she pleased. But ever since it was ratified, white supremacists, particularly members of the Ku Klux Klan, had been sabotaging the amendment by murdering hundreds of African Americans for voting, running for office, or just taking leading roles in their communities. This powerful form of intimidation was the norm throughout the South, tacitly endorsed by all the white-controlled state governments below the Mason-Dixon line. "The segregationists made it very difficult for black people to register," Parks said later, understating the case.

This type of coercion was facilitated by General Ulysses S. Grant's decision to allow the defeated Confederate soldiers to keep their rifles after the Civil War; as a result, southern blacks were not only outnumbered, but outarmed. A case in point is what happened in Colfax, Louisiana, in 1873, when a group of former slaves who considered themselves Lincoln Republicans held a public protest to demand that the Fifteenth Amendment be upheld. Their attempt at armed self-defense, however, ended in disaster: on Easter Sunday, 280 African Americans were slaughtered by vigilante bigots for daring to stand up to the white power structure. Three years later the situation became even worse when Republican Rutherford B. Hayes of Ohio was elected president—he withdrew federal troops from the South, thereby ending Reconstruction and stripping African Americans of the little armed protection they had.

But violence was only one of the tactics used to disfranchise African Americans after the Fifteenth Amendment became law and white Southerners could no longer simply deny blacks the vote. The bigots turned instead to outright fraud and legal loopholes to make it nearly impossible for blacks to meet the local voting qualifications required to register. Among the technicalities resorted to were grandfather clauses, literacy tests, and poll taxes too high for the South's poor blacks to afford. Another device for keeping blacks disfranchised was the "white primary," which claimed that political parties were voluntary organizations and therefore could discriminate in the primary elections that determined the party candidate. Blacks were also denied the vote by being convicted of bogus crimes. Routinely, African Americans were arrested on such absurd charges as insulting a white person, incarcerated, and then released with criminal records that made it impossible for them to register to vote. "The entire democratic process had been destroyed," Parks explained, to the point that "anyone, black or white—it didn't matter—who spoke out against segregation risked being killed."

The New Deal, however, gave African Americans hope that the South's vicious discriminatory practices might soon end. In fact, the Roosevelt administration appointed talented blacks to important, high-profile government posts, including educator and civil rights activist Mary McLeod Bethune, director of the Division of Negro Affairs of the National Youth Administration; economist Robert C. Weaver, an adviser to the Department of the Interior; and William H.

Hastie, a justice of the district court of the Virgin Islands and as such the first black federal judge in U.S. history. Although African Americans were grateful for the gesture and for the New Deal's help through the Great Depression, they viewed these token appointments as mainly symbolic.

When it came to voting rights, little progress was being made. In 1937 a group of poor voters brought a constitutional challenge against the poll tax that citizens were charged across the South for exercising their right to vote, and lost. The U.S. Supreme Court upheld the poll tax as constitutional. "If you were poor—which most blacks in Alabama were—and had no extra money, that meant you couldn't vote," Rosa Parks recalled.

It particularly rankled Parks that some African Americans proved willing to kowtow to whites for the privilege of registering to vote. "A small number of blacks who were in good favor with the white folks did get registered in that way," Parks recalled, "but once they got registered, they did not want other blacks to do the same. I guess they felt that when the white people vouched for and approved of them being registered, that put them on a different level from the rest of us." Her husband, Raymond, in fact, eventually quit the NAACP in frustration at the superior attitude some of the more educated blacks on Centennial Hill displayed toward rank-and-file workers like himself.

Rosa Parks's disgust at ballot-box discrimination grew after Japan bombed Pearl Harbor, Hitler's Germany declared war on the United States, and her baby brother, Sylvester, was drafted into the U.S. Army to risk his life defending a democracy in which he was unable to vote. This particularly outrageous injustice helped prompt Parks to join the

NAACP, which had successfully worked through the political and judicial establishments to outlaw grandfather clauses in 1915. During the war years, it focused on abolishing white primaries and literacy requirements for voting. "From the start the NAACP, to me at least, was about empowerment through the ballot box," Parks recalled. "With the vote would come economic improvements. We would have a voice."

It was Johnnie Mae Carr, Parks's old friend from Miss White's Industrial School for Girls, who inadvertently inspired her to sign up with the NAACP in December 1943, even after her husband, Raymond—who had joined in 1934—had quit the organization. As Parks explained, "I joined the NAACP after I saw Mrs. Johnnie Carr's picture in one of the papers," in an article in the *Alabama Tribune*, a black periodical. It was simple curiosity: she wanted to see whether this familiar-looking Mrs. Carr was in fact her old friend who had gone by the name Rebecca Daniels at Miss White's School. "She came to the program to see if I was the person she thought I was, and of course I was," Carr explained. Ironically, however, Parks failed to reunite with her old schoolmate that night; Carr did not attend the meeting. In fact, Parks was the only woman there, and as such was elected secretary of the chapter. "I was too timid to say no," Parks recalled. "I just started taking minutes."

Of course, she had other motivations to enlist, including her growing admiration for Walter White, whom Parks had read about in a glowing profile in *Look* magazine. Few African Americans championed the black cause as successfully as White. An insurance-company cashier by trade, in 1916 White had taken the lead in establishing an NAACP branch in his hometown of Atlanta; he served as the organization's assistant secretary from 1918 to 1931 and as executive secretary from 1931 to 1955. An ardent opponent of racial violence, he personally investigated eight race riots and more than forty lynchings. And when it came to desegregation, White was in a league of his own, articulating the injustice of Jim Crow to influential white Americans with an artfulness that hadn't been seen since Booker T. Washington. It was White's lobbying of the Roosevelts that helped bring about the establishment, in 1941, of the Fair Employment Practices Committee, which prohibited discrimination in defense industries; and his 1945 book *A Rising Wind* would serve as a prime catalyst behind President Harry S. Truman's decision to desegregate the armed forces.

One story Walter White liked to tell had a deep resonance for Rosa Parks, whose grandfather and husband were, like White, extremely light-skinned. "I am a Negro," as he explained in his autobiography *A Man Called White*, but "my skin is white, my eyes are blue, my hair is blond. The traits of my race are nowhere visible upon me." One afternoon he was standing on a subway platform in Harlem, waiting for a train to midtown. As it roared into the station, White stepped backward, accidentally planting his heel on the foot of a black man standing behind him. As White turned around to apologize, the man angrily snapped, "Why don't you look where you're going? You white folks are always trampling on colored people." At that moment, a friend of White's came up to him and asked how his fight in Washington, D.C., for a permanent Fair Employment Practices Committee was going. The man on whose toes White had stepped listened, then apologized. "Are you Walter White of the NAACP?"

he asked. "I'm sorry I spoke to you that way. I thought you were white."

To Parks, this story said it all about the silliness of the color line. The anecdote reminded her that many white Americans, such as civil rights activist Mary White Ovingston; NAACP founders Joel and Arthur Spingarn; Oswald Garrison Villard, owner of *The Nation*; and Chicago settlement house reformer Jane Addams had long championed full equality for black Americans. She also admired Walter White for choosing not to pass as white—for not being ashamed to be a Negro. And she liked the pragmatism with which he kept pushing for blacks' voting rights, making deals with everybody from Democratic U.S. senator Hugo L. Black of Alabama to Republican businessman Wendell Wilkie of New York. It was White's remarkable skill at coalition building that excited Parks, and she recognized that the NAACP under his leadership was beginning to blossom with a new vigor.

One of Parks's first assignments as local NAACP secretary was to help launch a voter registration drive, which proved no easy task. "In Montgomery in the 1940s we had what we called a Voters' League, a group of people who had meetings in each other's homes, mostly in our house," Parks recalled. "At that time I had a list of the black registered voters in Montgomery. There were thirty-one people on the registered list, and some of them were in the cemetery. They had died, but they were still on the list." The Montgomery NAACP chapter met monthly, usually on Sundays at various churches, to address community issues. The organization lacked the funds to rent office space, so the chapter's official headquarters was set up at executive secretary E. D. Nixon's modest, two-story redbrick home at 647 Clinton Avenue, just a few blocks from the Cleveland Courts projects.

It was Rosa Parks's great fortune to work with Edgar Daniel Nixon, a powerful, dark, bristling man with a hard-set brow and tight-end shoulders. Nixon was one of seventeen children; his father, a Baptist minister, was twice married. Born in Montgomery and raised in rural Alabama by his Aunt Pinky, a devout Seventh Day Adventist and strict disciplinarian, young E. D. received little formal schooling, and by age fourteen was supporting himself working in grocery stores and on the railroad line between Selma and Mobile. Nixon's greatest strength was also his biggest shortcoming: He was uneducated, unsophisticated, and expressed himself in the deep-throated slang idiom of the rural Black Belt.

In the estimation of Harrison Wofford, President John F. Kennedy's special assistant for civil rights, Nixon was a powerful force, a "Gandhi with guns," due to his penchant for brandishing firearms. Working-class blacks from West Montgomery respected his righteous brawn, while African-American professionals around Centennial Hills with degrees from southern black colleges like Atlanta's Morehouse and Spelman looked down on him as a gritty ward politician. "Some people thought Nixon was crude and rude," Parks remembered. "They were wrong. In the ways that matter—like manners—he was truly sophisticated."

But no one could argue that Nixon had grown into a brave and uncompromising crusader for equal rights. "He was a proud, dignified man who carried himself straight as an arrow," Parks recalled. He was also a male chauvinist given to muttering things like "Women don't need to be nowhere but in the kitchen." Parks openly challenged her boss for such sexist remarks; after all, if she were in a kitchen, she wouldn't be typing all his letters on her Underwood, organizing his lecture calendar, and answering his mail, all without pay. "Well, what about me?" she would retort, intimating that she might quit. And every time Nixon would back down, pleading, "But I need a secretary, and you are a good one."

What really distinguished E. D. Nixon from most African Americans in Montgomery was that he had traveled extensively as a railroad sleeping-car porter and had regularly visited the integrated North, where he ate with whites at New York diners and swam with them off the same Chicago beach on Lake Michigan. "Until I started working for the Pullman Company," Nixon explained, "I'd felt the whole world was like Montgomery. I figured if there was segregation here, there was segregation everywhere. I just didn't think about it."

It was a speech he heard on a stopover in St. Louis in 1927 that forever changed Nixon, and by so doing helped launch the modern civil rights movement. The regal black labor leader A. Philip Randolph, who had recently begun trying to organize Pullman workers into what would become the Brotherhood of Sleeping Car Porters, gave the speech at the YMCA where Nixon always stayed on his St. Louis runs. A handsome man of imposing size and dignity, Randolph had been raised in Florida and moved to New York, where he attended City College, joined the Socialist Party, and became coeditor of the *Messenger*, a pro-union magazine that also published black poets Langston Hughes, Countee Cullen, and Claude McKay. A relentless critic of the American Federation of Labor for the racist policies of its member unions,

Randolph went so far as to denounce American efforts in World War I, declaring in his rich baritone that instead of making "the world safe for democracy," the United States should "make Georgia safe for the Negro."

For twelve years, Randolph challenged the Pullman Company—the largest employer of blacks in the nation—to scrap its anti-black-union policies, eventually winning his crusade in 1937. "Nothing counts but pressure, pressure, more pressure, and still more pressure through broad, organized, aggressive mass action," Randolph would teach an entirely new generation of civil rights activists. When Nixon encountered Randolph, the silver-tongued activist was urging Pullman porters to ally with him to fight for guaranteed raises in salary to $150 a month. Nixon, who was making only $72.50 a month, was stunned by his temerity. "When I heard Randolph talk the first time, I had never heard a black man talk like that before," Nixon recalled. "Let me tell you, that guy could talk."

Nixon, dressed in his white Pullman uniform, dutifully dropped a dollar in the collection plate, returned to Montgomery a union man, and in 1928 helped his new mentors Walter White and Roy Wilkins establish state and local NAACP chapters in Alabama. During the Great Depression, Nixon organized the Montgomery Welfare League to help poor blacks get on the welfare rolls, and in 1941 he joined forces with Randolph to plan a national march on Washington by one hundred thousand African Americans to protest racial discrimination in the U.S. defense industry, a threat that forced President Franklin D. Roosevelt to issue the executive order establishing the Fair Employment Practices

Committee. "Oh boy did Mr. Nixon look up to Mr. Randolph," Parks later laughed. "He was more than an idol, he was an inspiration to him."

Starting in 1943, Rosa Parks would spend a lot of free time at Nixon's residential office, tucked away under a garage awning, hidden from public view. The top of the house had two small-windowed turrets, which gave the dwelling the appearance of modest wealth. There were banana trees and scraggly cactus in the neighborhood that made Clinton Avenue seem as if it belonged in Tampa or Tallahassee. The two front windows had ornate black metal bars in front for protection from vandals. A wonderful typist and organizer, Parks kept the home office running when Nixon was on his long runs up the Eastern seaboard or to the Midwest stockyards. Nixon saw himself as the champion of the poor, the voiceless. The two pressing issues Parks dealt with from this hideaway were voting rights and desegregation of the city buses, both among the Jim Crow issues that most concerned Montgomery's blacks.

During this period Montgomery's African-American community was divided between middle-class professionals, who lived around Centennial Hill, and the poorer working-class residents of the city's west side. To help mobilize a united, citywide voter registration drive, Nixon—who had taken to carrying a pistol to city hall just in case—organized the Alabama Voters' League in 1943, enlisting the legal assistance of Arthur A. Madison, an Alabama native who had become a civil rights attorney in Harlem. In her autobiography, My Story, Parks recounts how Madison had returned to Montgomery determined to spearhead a mass action against disfranchisement. The fiery Madison informed the Montgomery NAACP and the Alabama Voters' League that blacks didn't need whites to vouch for their right to vote and that the literacy requirement, which demanded that blacks who wanted to register have basic reading and writing skills, was unconstitutional. For these heresies the Montgomery police labeled Madison not only an unwelcome outsider but an anti-American troublemaker bent on undermining the city's social codes. That summer, Madison was arrested for so-called barratry when his niece, Sarah Pearl Madison, a schoolteacher, testified against him for invoking her name in a voting-registration case without her consent. Madison was eventually released from jail but was disbarred from practicing law in Alabama for representing a person without authorization. Under court order he returned to New York, abandoning his Alabama voting rights crusade forever.

Nevertheless, Madison's passion, combined with Nixon's courage, made a convert of Rosa Parks. She was disgusted that the Montgomery branch of the NAACP had not fought harder for Madison once he was arrested. "I decided to get registered," she put it simply. "The first year I tried was 1943." She quickly discovered that exercising her right as an American meant surmounting a series of deliberate bureaucratic obstacles. For example, the state would open its voter-registration rolls only at certain times—without publicly announcing what those times were. Often the window of opportunity would be scheduled between 10 A.M. and noon, when most white employers refused to let their black employees off work. If African Americans showed up, anyway, state officials would move the line so slowly that only a handful of would-be voters made it in to register before the doors closed; everyone else in line was told to wait until next time.

The few blacks who got into the office were ridiculed for failing to own property and forced to take a literacy test.

Parks tried to register twice in 1943, but to no avail. While whites received their voter certificates when they registered, blacks had to wait for theirs in the mail—and Parks's never came. After many inquiries, she was finally informed that she had failed her literacy test. Refusing to give in to discouragement, Parks queued up to take the test again in 1944, and again was flatly rejected. "They just told me, 'You didn't pass,'" she recalled. "They didn't have to give you a reason."

Rosa Parks grew justifiably frustrated and resentful, constantly praying to God to guide her through this vexatious ordeal. Yet her inner resolve never wavered, and her sense of purpose remained defiantly unflappable. Throughout the humiliating process she clung to the lesson in Luke 18, that persistence to excess can wear away even the sturdiest walls of marble. She also remembered Frederick Douglass's plea that "the Negro be not judged by the heights to which he is risen, but by the depths from which he has climbed" and felt blessed to be thirty-one years old, happily married, healthy, well-off enough to take care of her frail mother, and supported by the St. Paul AME Church of Montgomery as her sanctuary and guide. As a Christian, she knew it would be wrong to let Jim Crow break her spirit or to allow any prejudice against whites, however justified, to defile the gospel of love for her. Instead, she would turn to 1 Corinthians 12:13: "For by one spirit we were all baptized into one body, whether Jews, Greeks, whether slaves or free, and we are all made to drink of one Spirit." Parks also drew inspiration from Tuscumbia, Alabama, native Helen Keller, the first deaf and blind person to earn a college degree and with it world renown as America's "First Lady of Courage."

But when Parks made a second attempt to vote one gray November afternoon in 1943, her studied serenity and patience were sorely tested by a bigoted bus driver named James F. Blake, who would play an even larger role in her life a dozen years later. Out of all the Jim Crow laws, those segregating buses were the most complex and arbitrary. With water fountains the apartheid code was simple: One was marked "colored," the other "whites." But every bus system in the South seemed to follow a byzantine set of rules, made more confusing by the whims of individual drivers. In Montgomery, for example, all of the city's buses had thirty-six seats, the first ten always reserved for whites. The ten seats farthest toward the back of the buses were unofficially designated for the use of African Americans, provided white passengers didn't need them. As for the sixteen seats in between, individual drivers imposed their own segregation rules at random and enforced them with the threat of the pistols they carried. This inconsistency of oppression in the Montgomery bus system only added to the unfairness toward black riders, who learned to forgo the middle seats or at least to give them up to any white person if asked. Many drivers enhanced the degradation by making blacks pay their fares through the front door, then get off and go around to the back of the bus to board. It was a form of everyday public humiliation in apartheid Montgomery. "Some bus drivers were meaner than others," Parks related. "Not all of them were hateful, but segregation itself is vicious, and to my mind there was no way you could make segregation decent or nice or acceptable."

Not that James F. Blake had any intentions in that direction. Blake was a vicious bigot who spat tobacco juice out of his bus window and cursed at "nigras" just for the fun of it. "He just treated everybody black badly," Parks remembered; his favorite sport was making African Americans pay in front and walk back to board in the rear, then leaving them with a faceful of exhaust as he gunned the bus away before they could get on. Black women were prime targets for his slurs of "bitch" and "coon." Rosa Parks never could understand the depth of Blake's malignity, but she knew evil in the Christian sense when she saw it.

On that November afternoon in 1943, when she boarded through the front door because every seat and place to stand in the back of the bus was crammed with African Americans, Parks knew she might be in for an ugly encounter. Sure enough, the driver glared at her, hand near the holster on his hip, and demanded that she exit the bus and reboard it through the back door. "I told him I was already on the bus and didn't see the need of getting off and getting back on when people were standing in the stepwell, and how was I going to squeeze in, anyway?" Parks still fumed decades later. "So he told me if I couldn't go through the back door that I would have to get off the bus—'my bus,' he called it. I stood where I was."

This first encounter with Blake has often been overlooked by historians. The square-off's importance, however, cannot be denied, for it was the same James F. Blake who was driving the Cleveland Avenue bus twelve years later when Parks once again refused to budge, with far greater consequences. In the dozen years after her first taste of his bigotry, out of pride she never boarded a bus that Blake was driving. Textbook accounts of her momentous stand of December 1, 1955, generally neglect to mention that the drama unfolded in large part because Parks had absentmindedly boarded Blake's bus that day, and that her act of civil disobedience was partly the result of her personal revulsion toward one particular bus driver.

Her refusal to capitulate to Blake's request in 1943 foreshadowed her future significance in another way as well. When Blake began tugging on Parks's coat sleeve to push her physically off the bus, she did not struggle. She held her head high and warned him not to strike her; she would exit of her own accord. Startled, all Blake could manage in reply was an enraged "Get off my bus," to which Parks responded by intentionally dropping her handbag and then plopping down on a whites-only seat to retrieve it on her way out, further infuriating the driver.

Intuitively, Parks had engaged in an act of passive resistance, a precept named by Leo Tolstoy and embraced by Mahatma Gandhi but drawn from the New Testament Parks knew so well. She had learned from Matthew 5:39 of Jesus' teaching that if an adversary slaps you on one cheek, you should turn the other. Although she took the lesson to heart and understood that it meant the victim should turn the aggressor on a higher road, Parks was not about to tolerate being slapped on her cheek or anywhere else by James Blake or anyone else. As Parks read the New Testament, Jesus had been speaking metaphorically, for when he was slapped on an occasion described in John 18:23, he renounced the offender. Thus, Parks not only refused to get back on Blake's bus; she avoided him for the next twelve years, opting to walk home in the rain rather than suffer further injustice at the hands of a bully.

Parks's resistance to Jim Crow persisted, and at least on the voting question it paid off. In April 1945, just weeks after FDR had died in Warm Springs, Georgia, and with E. D. Nixon at her side, Rosa Parks tried to register to vote at Montgomery's city hall and for a third time was forced to take a literacy test. "I made a copy of my answers to those twenty-one questions," Parks related. "They didn't have copy machines in those days. I copied them by hand. I was going to keep that copy and use it to bring suit against the voter registration board." She was relieved when it turned out she didn't have to go to such lengths: She received her voter certificate in the mail. But even so, another obstacle remained to be overcome. To actually vote, Parks had to pay a poll tax of $16.50—a hefty sum for a full-time clerk who barely made ends meet by doubling as a part-time seamstress. And there was other good news: in December 1945, in a nasty square-off, Nixon defeated the incumbent NAACP Montgomery branch president for his job. Nixon and Parks were now the team in charge.

Parks cast her very first vote for James "Big Jim" Folsom in the 1946 Alabama governor's race. A colorful populist from Coffee County in the southeastern corner of the state known as the Wiregrass, Folsom told funny anecdotes, sang Carter Family anthems like "Keep on the Sunny Side," railed against the elites he called "Big Mules," and championed equal rights for women and blacks. It thrilled both Rosa and Raymond Parks to hear Big Jim Folsom denouncing Klan night riders and greedy, rich white folks. A true maverick, their candidate had no campaign manager, no headquarters, and no financial backing. But Folsom did have seasoned New Dealer Aubrey Williams at his side, a man conservatives excoriated as an atheist, a Kremlin Communist, a "nigger lover," and "the most dangerous man in America." When Folsom pulled off the upset and was elected governor of Alabama, Rosa and Raymond Parks joined more than one hundred thousand others to cheer at his inaugural parade. As fate would have it, both Folsom and Williams would play key roles in the Montgomery bus boycott nine years later.

In the wake of Folsom's victory, Rosa Parks became disenchanted. Though she had worked so hard for the right to vote and had seen her candidate win, Jim Crow continued to rule Montgomery even with Big Jim in the governor's mansion. Still, she had won an important personal battle, a success she credited to the NAACP, which had grown in stature after helping to end the bloody race riots in Detroit and Harlem in 1943. By 1946, the organization counted 1,073 branches and a membership of some 450,000. World War II had pushed the NAACP's public-relations operation into overdrive, including national promotion of the Double V Campaign, to signify victory against racism both at home and abroad. Unfortunately, the victory never came, as Rosa Parks saw firsthand when her brother returned home in 1945 a war hero—and was greeted with derision by white Alabamans, who objected to the very idea of African Americans in uniform, no matter how many of their sons' lives the black soldiers may have saved.

Chapter 4

Laying a Foundation

THERE IS A PHOTO of Rosa's younger brother, Sylvester Mc-
Cauley, eyebrows arched in skepticism, his trim mustache
perfectly bisecting his face, meticulous in his U.S. Army uniform. Assigned to the 1318th Medical Detachment's Engi-
neering Services Regiment, Sylvester served in both the
European and Pacific theaters. During the war his young
bride, Daisy, gave birth to their first son—Sylvester junior—
in Gaffney, South Carolina, where they had met when he
was in training. He was a medic during the Battle of Normandy and later sailed out of San Francisco for the South
Seas. In a moving letter written from postwar Okinawa on
September 20, 1945, to his mother, Leona, Sylvester apolo-
gizes for being out of communication since the bombing of
Hiroshima and inquires about his beautiful older sister, Rosa.
As a private first-class in the army, Sylvester, a stretcher-
bearer, had seen the horrors of war close up and witnessed
countless soldiers die on blood-drenched battlefields, in
makeshift ambulances, and at military hospitals. He longed
to return home to his sweet Alabama, where his two children
were learning to walk and talk and Johnny Shines still sang
the blues. The NAACP's Double V Campaign had captured
Sylvester's imagination, and from half a world away he believed in the birth of a new era of racial harmony in the

South and that the manacles of Alabama's bigotry would disappear just as surely as Hitler in his German bunker. It turned out to be a pipe dream.

Sylvester returned to a South seething with racial animosity, especially toward black servicemen. Ninety percent of Southern Baptist churches turned their backs on black soldiers seeking to pray. During the war German prisoners of war laboring in the fields of the Mississippi Delta were sometimes fed at local cafés. The Nazis entered through the front door; their black American guards were forced to enter through the back. While stationed in Europe, some black soldiers had married Italian or French women. In Alabama, looking the wrong way at a white woman could be fatal. Even in death whites and blacks remain segregated—in funeral homes, in cemeteries, and even in death notices in local newspapers. "The treatment accorded the Negro during the Second World War marks, for me, a turning point in the Negro's relation in America," James Baldwin explained in *The Fire Next Time*. "To put it briefly, and somewhat too simply, a certain hope died, a certain respect for white Americans faded."

Half a million black soldiers saw duty in Europe and the Pacific; another half million served their nation stateside, nearly 9 percent of the total U.S. forces. All blacks were segregated in units under white command, as their fathers had been a quarter of a century earlier in World War I. Black servicemen returning to the South were met with the humiliation of Jim Crow, the vitriol of Dixiecrat politicians, and the brutality of the Klan. Lieutenant Robert Powell, an African-American Silver Star recipient, summed it up best—"A soldier was looked on as a hero if he had medals on his chest, but still it was the back of the bus for us." Shown a photo of black soldiers dancing with Bavarian women, Alvin Owsley, former commander of the American Legion, warned Supreme Allied Commander Dwight D. Eisenhower: "I do not know . . . where these Negroes come from, but it is likely, if they expect to return to the South, they are on their way to be hanged or to be burned alive at public lynchings by the white men of the South."

Owsley's warning was prophetic. Violent assaults against black veterans occurred with startling frequency throughout the South. "[M]y very stomach turned over when I learned that Negro soldiers just back from overseas were being dumped out of army trucks and beaten," President Harry Truman exclaimed. A mob in Monroe, Georgia, murdered four blacks, including a uniformed veteran. One case particularly rankled Rosa Parks. In 1946, Sergeant Isaac Woodward, on his first furlough after fifteen months in the South Pacific, boarded an interstate bus in Georgia. The driver, perceiving the confident sergeant as uppity, berated him for taking too long in a "colored only" rest room at a South Carolina station. The driver phoned the sheriff in the next town, and when the bus arrived, Woodward, a teetotaler, was arrested for public intoxication. Using a blackjack and nightstick, the police beat Woodward into unconsciousness. Woodward was convicted, fined fifty dollars, and tossed into jail. His injuries were so severe—ribs shattered and coughing blood—that he was eventually taken to the military hospital in Spartanburg, South Carolina. Woodward's corneas were so badly damaged that he was deemed permanently blind. The Woodward tragedy—and others like it—deeply gnawed at Rosa Parks.

Sylvester's return to civilian life in Christmas 1945 was not greeted with honor but heaped with indignities. He was spat on by rednecks, declared "uppity" by the local police, and refused a job in Montgomery. It infuriated Rosa, indeed tormented her, that her brother, a gallant soldier who had saved white lives during the war, was regarded as an undesirable, a troublemaker, solely because of his skin color. He had become a true Invisible Man. "A lot of black World War II veterans came back and tried to get registered to vote and could not," Parks recalls. "They found they were treated with even more disrespect, especially if they were in uniform. Whites felt that things should remain as they had always been and that the black veterans were getting too sassy. My brother was one who could not take that kind of treatment anymore."

Sylvester was not about to waste his life waiting for the South to change. With his wife and two children—Sylvester junior and Mary—in tow, he headed up Highway 61 to Detroit for a janitorial job at a Chrysler factory. "He never went back to Alabama after he left," Rosa recalled. "He never visited at all." Sylvester was one of thousands of black Alabamans who swarmed into Detroit to find work. Although the Motor City was teeming with opportunity, postwar economic discrimination against blacks was widespread. In June 1948, for example, nearly 65 percent of all job openings in Detroit contained antiblack provisions, with "White Workers Preferred" announcements commonplace. None of Detroit's large retail businesses employed blacks as salesclerks. Throughout the Truman era not a single Detroit black was employed to drive private buses, interstate trucks, or white-owned taxicabs.

Even black nurses were shunned at city hospitals. This was no promised land, but still, the auto industry provided many African Americans with meaningful employment.

A few months after Sylvester settled in Detroit, Rosa came for a two-week visit—her first trip out of Alabama. Initially she marveled at how integrated Detroit was, a metropolis famous since the Civil War as the last stop on the Underground Railroad before runaway slaves escaped into Canada. "You could find a seat anywhere on a bus," Rosa reveled. "You could get better accommodations in Detroit." Sylvester took Rosa on a drive in his Ford Plymouth down Woodward Avenue, eight lanes starting at the Detroit River and proceeding for eight miles to the city limits. As she was chaperoned around downtown—visiting the Detroit Art Institute and General Motors' Fischer Building—she felt freer than ever before. But Montgomery ran in her veins. In Detroit she couldn't get the simple pleasures that made life in Montgomery so special: Merritt's Beaten Biscuits and Buffalo Rock ginger ale, WCOV-AM radio and gospel Sundays at St. Paul AME, soul lunch at the Ben Moore Hotel's rooftop restaurant and collard greens at the local market, and she was unenthusiastic about coping with Lake Erie snow and the Ontario cold. She was impressed with Detroit's Second Baptist Church—where, according to legend, the signing of the Emancipation Proclamation was first celebrated—but the homegirl in her missed the joyful shouts of "Oh, yes," "That's right preacher," "Uh-huh," and "You can say that again, brother!" from the beloved AME congregation back home. But the capper was the numerous shocking stories Rosa heard about Detroit's race riots of 1943.

The rapid migration of more than half a million job seekers resulted in substandard housing, high rates of tuberculosis and infant mortality, and simmering racial tensions that sparked one of the worst race riots in American history. In February 1943 a white mob attacked several black tenants at the Sojourner Truth housing project in Detroit. By June 20 the tensions exploded into mass riots started by a fracas at an amusement park. Thirty-four blacks and nine whites died, and thousands of both races were injured. Entire city blocks were destroyed while Detroit's mayor and Michigan's governor were paralyzed by fear and indecision. Vicious bands of white youths roamed the streets, beating every black they could catch, and soon the blacks began to reciprocate. Wartime factory production ground to a halt, but the governor tried to prevent federal troops from entering the city in hopes that his state forces could control the situation. After a week of sporadic rioting, looting, and arson, however, he relented and allowed President Roosevelt to send two military police battalions into Detroit. There wasn't much left for them to do, for by then both sides had grown weary of the violence, and the disorder came to an end. Rosa came to realize that Detroit was not an oasis of tolerance. "Racism was almost as widespread in Detroit as in Montgomery," she later told a radio interviewer. "And my husband, Raymond, wanted to stay in Alabama. So we put aside any ideas of moving to a northern promised land that wasn't."

In the beginning, Rosa Parks, who had stayed in the Deep South to fight Jim Crow, was not a grassroots organizer or a front-line fighter. Instead, she worked behind the scenes—as a record keeper, tallying local membership payments to send to the national NAACP headquarters in Washington, D.C., and writing letters on behalf of E. D. Nixon when he became Montgomery branch president in 1945 and 1946, then state president in 1947. From a newly opened NAACP office on Monroe Street she scanned journals like *The Crisis* and *Dissent* for newsworthy items for Alabama's black state newspaper, the *Birmingham World,* and issued regular press releases to the *Montgomery Advertiser* and occasionally to the *Atlanta Constitution.* While the NAACP's executives made dinner speeches and attended national conventions, Rosa balanced the ledgers, kept the books, and recorded every report of racial discrimination that crossed her desk. She also did field research, traveling from towns like Union Springs to cities like Selma to interview African Americans with legal complaints, including some who had witnessed the murders of blacks by whites in rural areas.

It was on a trip to an NAACP leadership-training seminar in Jacksonville, Florida in 1946 that Parks met the indomitable Ella Baker, a former field secretary who had risen to become national director of the NAACP's branch offices. A native of Virginia, the inwardly rebellious Baker, an avatar for participatory democracy, was as unlikely a civil rights organizer as Parks. According to Julian Bond, who worked closely with Baker in the 1960s, there was "something pleasingly prim and benignly schoolmarmish" about her. Often working with only men in Montgomery—many of whom were chauvinistic—Parks felt lonely for female camaraderie. But her encounter with Ella Baker, whom she found "beautiful in every way," filled her with a new sense of purpose. "She was so smart and funny and strong," Parks recalled of the NAACP's top woman executive at the time. "After Jacksonville, whenever she came to Montgomery, she stayed with me. She was a true friend—a mentor, I'd guess you'd say. We often exchanged letters."

Bolstered by Baker, Parks's own stature began to grow in the civil rights community. By the October 1947 NAACP Alabama state convention, her reputation got her named to the three-person nominating committee that recommended that Emory O. Jackson, a Birmingham insurance salesman, step down as state president in favor of E. D. Nixon. Never known for oratory, Parks surprised everybody the following year when she spoke passionately at the state NAACP convention in Mobile. Rising to the occasion, Parks quoted the Bible and Booker T. Washington, decried the mistreatment of African-American women across the Black Belt, and chided those dandies who used the annual convention as an occasion for southern boosterism. "No one should feel proud of a place," she said, "as long as Negroes are intimidated." She received thunderous applause, and the convention appointed her secretary of the statewide NAACP conference, on top of her position as secretary of the organization's Montgomery branch. "I was nervous to death," Parks recalled of the speech. "But the entire Mobile experience gave me self-confidence."

It is a great loss to civil rights historiography that Parks's NAACP files, which had been put in a shed for safekeeping, were inadvertently thrown out by a friend of E. D. Nixon's in the 1960s. "A great deal of history was lost, because we kept notes on many cases," Parks recalled. "But we didn't have too many successes in getting justice. It was more a matter of trying to challenge the powers that be and to let it be known that we did not wish to continue being treated as second-class citizens." As a result, forever missing from the historical record is the documentation of the NAACP's Montgomery activity from 1943 to 1950—the year Nixon was replaced as branch president. Parks was no prose stylist, but she set out the search for justice in concise memoranda and meeting minutes. And in 1952, when Nixon was elected as president of the Montgomery chapter of the Progressive Democratic Association—the voice of Alabama's black Democrats— Parks continued to work for him for free.

Her paying job during this period was at Crittenden's Tailor Shop at 42 Perry Street, where she altered custom-fit men's suits and handsewed dresses to the exacting precision of the fine seamstress she was. Her office skills exhibited the same meticulousness: she proofread every document before it left her desk as if history depended on it. Parks took a particular interest in certain egregious rape cases, including one in which a black woman from Abbeville, Alabama—Rosa's father's hometown—had been kidnapped on her way home from church, forced into a car at gunpoint, and stripped naked and gang-raped by six white men. Rosa monitored the case closely. When a Henry County grand jury failed to indict the men, Rosa helped to spur the NAACP to pressure Governor Chauncey Sparks to convene a special grand jury. Again the rapists were not indicted, but she never gave up.

Parks also took up the cause of the framed Jeremiah Reeves, an eighteen-year-old grocery delivery boy who was invited into the home of one of his customers, a white woman, for a little afternoon romance. A nosy neighbor who happened to be peering into the bedroom window witnessed the pair undressing. When the white woman realized her neighbor had found her out, as in the famous scene from

Harper Lee's novel *To Kill a Mockingbird*, she cried rape. While the Montgomery NAACP branch worked to free Reeves, Parks corresponded with him personally to keep his spirits up, and even helped the so-called rapist get the poetry he wrote in prison published in the *Birmingham World*. Again, however, the efforts were to no avail: After spending years on death row, Reeves was executed in the electric chair on March 28, 1958, despite pleas for clemency by Martin Luther King, Jr., and others to Governor James Folsom.

Such defeats might have crushed most people, but Rosa persisted. In 1949, she became adviser to the informal NAACP Youth Group that grew into the organization's official Youth Council in 1953. Childless and far from her nieces and nephews in Detroit, she adopted her neighborhood's youngsters as her own, serving as a sort of special aunt or guidance counselor. Never did Parks seem happier or more at ease than when reading passages from *Uncle Tom's Cabin* to a gaggle of wide-eyed ten-year-olds or organizing spelling bees at the local church for ambitious high schoolers. She taught them all how to maintain a sense of dignity in a Jim Crow town. As E. D. Nixon later recalled: "Kids just love Mrs. Parks to death. They had a special bond, an understanding, that was very rare indeed, full of hugs and all that."

The NAACP Youth Council was not a Scout-like organization; it was a precursor to the highly politicized, activist Student Nonviolent Coordinating Committee (SNCC, pronounced "Snick"), founded in 1960 by Ella Baker to synchronize sit-in demonstrations on college campuses. The Youth Council, under the leadership of Nixon, Parks, and others, launched a desegregation campaign at Montgomery's main library at South McDonough Street. The city's colored libraries had an almost nonexistent budget, with few books. A group of students, coached by Nixon and Parks, walked into the main library requesting service. "They did this again and again," Parks lamented, "but they were unsuccessful in changing the practice." The youths did, however, begin to gain confidence in their own voices.

In the little free time left between her job and her work for the NAACP, Rosa made herself a regular presence at St. Paul AME Church. The wood-framed Hardaway Street sanctuary had burned down in 1933, and Rosa helped spearhead an effort to erect a new one. The congregation temporarily rented space at Tullibody Hall on the campus of Alabama State University. A year later, thanks to an overwhelmingly successful fund-raising drive, a new redbrick edifice was opened on Hall Street, just across the street from the university. Due to its central location, St. Paul AME became a spiritual way station for out-of-town preachers. AME clergy throughout the South, in fact, played a crucial role in the civil rights movement, one that has been obscured because Martin Luther King and Ralph Abernathy were Baptists. J. A. Delaine, an AME pastor and school principal in Clarendon County, South Carolina, and Oliver Brown, pastor of St. Mark AME Church in Topeka, Kansas, filed the two most famous suits against public-school segregation. In later years Parks would remember how inspired she was to hear civil rights sermons from the pulpit of her own church. A stalwart member of St. Paul AME, Rosa taught Sunday School at 9:30 A.M. and served as stewardess for the 10:30 A.M. service, preparing the elements for the Lord's Supper—bread and wine—and making sure there was a white linen cloth to place them on. She considered St. Paul AME her "special living room," and she became even more involved in 1953 under the pastorate of the Reverend Henry Duncombe—a master spinner of parables and riddles—when the church underwent a renovation program, expanding its space by two thousand square feet.

In 1950, E. D. Nixon lost the chapter election and relinquished his position as head of the Montgomery NAACP to victor Robert L. Matthews. By that point Rosa Parks—who had resigned as branch secretary in May 1949 to attend to her ailing mother—had become more of a freelance assistant to Nixon than an official NAACP staffer. The Brotherhood of Sleeping Car Porters had given her boss a union office on Monroe Street, right near the downtown NAACP headquarters, and after Parks completed a long workday sewing at the Crittenden's Tailor Shop, where she earned about twenty-five dollars a week, she often made her way to Nixon's cluttered office to answer his mail, file paperwork, and return telephone calls. Since Nixon was often traveling the country, away sometimes for two-week stretches, he needed Rosa to keep his activist life in order. She even brought him supper on backlogged nights and advised him as to which tie best matched each shirt and Brooks Brothers suit.

After a two-year absence from the NAACP, Parks returned in early 1952—her mother's health stabilized—to once again serve as branch secretary. A slight rift had developed between Parks and Nixon because he wanted her to continue working solely in his Brotherhood office. "Every day in the early 1950s we were looking for ways to challenge Jim Crow laws," Parks recalled. "I stayed in close touch with the other NAACP offices." A turning point in the civil rights struggle took place in Louisiana in June 1953, one that excited Parks immensely. Blacks in Baton Rouge had been conducting a weeklong boycott of city buses under the leadership of the Reverend T. J. Jemison of Mt. Zion Baptist Church. The showdown had been set the summer before, when Baton Rouge's city council passed Ordinance 222 authorizing an integrationist "first-come, first-served" bus-seating policy. This progressive measure was immediately challenged by an outraged group of Louisiana whites who charged Mayor Jesse L. Webb, Jr., with pandering to black voters and being a lackey of the NAACP. The bus drivers, who had been stripped of their authority over who sat where, were particularly incensed. Tensions were roiling by June 1953, when a black passenger refused to give up his seat to a white man one day. The bus driver headed straight to a police station and demanded that the "Negro troublemaker" be arrested. While the police sided with the white passenger and driver, when the issue came before the mayor, Webb said the black passenger was in the right. In other words, Ordinance 222 was no joke; open bus seating was the new policy in Baton Rouge.

Pandemonium broke out citywide in response. Angry bus drivers went on strike, blaming the NAACP for inciting racial strife. "That Negro outfit is . . . telling Negroes they have a right to sit anywhere they want and advising them not to move," sputtered the secretary of the drivers' union. Anxious to quell the strike, Louisiana's attorney general weighed in on the side of the drivers, saying that Ordinance 222 was illegal because it violated the state's segregation laws. The vindicated drivers returned to work, eager to reimpose the old Jim Crow system and jubilant that they had muzzled

the glory-seeking Reverend Jemison—whose "racial opportunism" they demonized as "Communist-inspired."

They crowed too soon. Instead of capitulating, Baton
Rouge's black churches created a United Defense League
(UDL) to direct a citywide bus boycott, a forerunner of the
Montgomery bus boycott two and a half years later. A UDL
spokesperson made a radio appeal to all blacks not to ride
city buses. At a June 19 rally Reverend Jemison, a Selma, Alabama, preacher whose father was president of the 5-million-
member National Baptist Convention, the largest black
organization in the United States, pointed out that "it's illegal to boycott," so "we're just not riding."

The boycott was an immediate success, costing Baton
Rouge's bus company $1,600 a day in lost revenue and em-
boldening Jemison to present a laundry list of demands, including the hiring of black bus drivers. But for reasons still
unclear, just as the boycott was beginning to sting, on June
25 Jemison called it off in acquiescence to a foolish compromise measure: Ordinance 251, which reserved the two front
seats for whites and the long backseat for blacks, with open
seating on the rest. Many on the front lines of the boycott
felt that Jemison had sold them down the river, a point he
admitted when he frankly stated that it was premature to
abolish segregation. "You cannot change traditions and customs overnight," he claimed wanly.

From his vantage point in Montgomery, E. D. Nixon
agreed that the African-American citizens of Baton Rouge
had been "let down" by a timid Jemison and "tricked" by
their city council. Yet for the two weeks in June that it lasted,
both Nixon and Parks monitored the boycott obsessively,

thrilling that Louisiana blacks had so quickly mobilized en masse for equal rights, held rousing rallies eight thousand strong, created a car-pool system that worked, and most important, sent a message to America via peaceful civil disobedience that *Plessy v. Ferguson* was profoundly and totally antidemocratic. Without outside financial assistance, Baton Rouge blacks inaugurated the direct action phase of the struggle for civil rights in the South, and their bus boycott became an invaluable case study for Martin Luther King, Jr., Ralph Abernathy, and other leaders who would launch their own bus boycott in Montgomery courtesy of Rosa Parks in 1955. "In 1892, Homer Plessy refused to sit in a Jim Crow railroad car, and the Supreme Court ruled against him," Parks recalled. "Baton Rouge was—like the Montgomery bus boycott—an organized attempt to vindicate Homer Plessy."

One reason historians have downplayed the significance of the Baton Rouge boycott is that less than a year later the Supreme Court overturned the legal underpinning of Jim Crow, *Plessy v. Ferguson*, sending shock waves throughout the South. On May 17, 1954—the most important day for black Americans since Abraham Lincoln delivered the Emancipation Proclamation—in a unanimous decision known as *Brown v. Board of Education*, a Topeka case, Chief Justice Earl Warren rejected the long-standing *Plessy* doctrine, declaring that separate public schools were "inherently unequal" because state-sanctioned segregation violated the Fourteenth Amendment's guarantee of equal protection under the law. Shortly after handing down its landmark verdict the Supreme Court issued implementation guidelines ordering the federal district courts to supervise school desegregation "on a racially nondiscriminatory basis with all deliberate speed." Resistance to the *Brown* decision sprang up immediately and virulently among many white southerners, whose distaste manifested itself in the formation of the White Citizens' Council in Mississippi, an organization that soon spread across the region. Nevertheless, the South's blacks brimmed with optimism. "You can't imagine the rejoicing among black people, and some white people, when the Supreme Court decision came down in May 1954," Parks enthused in *My Story*. "It was a very hopeful time."

There is a black-and-white photograph of Nixon and Parks sitting together at a long conference table, taken in 1954 at the NAACP Montgomery chapter's annual meeting, the first since the Brown decision and the Baton Rouge bus boycott. Of the thirty people present, Nixon and Parks stand out. Dignified, his giant hands resting on his knees, Nixon is clearly the leader of the convocation, exuding the self-confidence of a man with a mission. Parks, resplendent in her blouse and jacket, stands out because she is a woman and because she radiates an unmistakable sense of inner strength. About Montgomery, which she called Jeffersonville in a short story, the southern belle Zelda Fitzgerald once wrote, "Every place has its hour . . . a time and quality that appertains to nowhere else." A faded snapshot in Rosa Parks's Detroit archive is a relic of that hour when Montgomery was in the eye of a hurricane of community action that would change America forever.

CHAPTER 5

The Preparation

As Rosa Parks's activism grew, her dormant feminism also flourished. Like most African-American women of the time—60 percent in 1950—Parks worked part-time as a domestic seamstress and housekeeper for better-off white families, but she flatly refused to be Mammy-fied into the servile, grinning stereotype of the black female.

The educator Barbara Omolade described, in her 1994 book *The Rising Song of African American Women*, how domestic service required black housemaids to become quite intimate with their white mistresses, the better to "fit into" their households, carry out their whims, and accede to working long hours, including on weekends and holidays. Domestic servitude—as poet Maya Angelou detailed in her fine autobiography, *I Know Why the Caged Bird Sings*—encompassed everything from scrubbing toilets to raising children, from sewing clothes to pulling weeds to polishing silver, all for very low pay. Novelist Zora Neale Hurston summed up the state of things in *Their Eyes Were Watching God*: "De nigger woman is de mule uh de world as fur as Ah can see." And so she was treated. Many white ladies of the house called their black domestics by generic names like "Mary" or "Suzie," as one would a pet. As William Faulkner put it in *The Sound and the Fury*, to her white mistress Mrs. Compson, the mammy figure Dilsey is "a blobby shape without depth." It was Rosa Parks's good fortune that the white family she worked for as a seamstress in 1954 and 1955 was that of Clifford and Virginia Foster Durr.

Virginia Foster had been raised in the antebellum customs of Old Birmingham, carefully trained to become a gracious debutante who was naturally elected vice president of the city's Junior League. But this creature of Old South privilege attended Miss Finch's Finishing School in New York, the Cathedral School in Washington, D.C., and Wellesley College in Massachusetts, dropping out her sophomore year because she was unable to afford the tuition. (The boll-weevil plague had devastated cotton production, and the family fortune had dwindled.) Perhaps because of her northern exposure and education, unlike most of the Birmingham society set, Foster developed a social conscience that was repulsed by the South's racial caste system. In Studs Terkel's classic oral history of the Great Depression, *Hard Times*, Virginia Foster Durr remembered the faces of poor black children stricken with rickets and pellagra and how whites would rather pour unneeded milk down the gutter than give it to malnourished Negroes. This experience inspired the socialite to devote her life to helping the downtrodden.

It was her marriage in 1926 to Clifford J. Durr of Montgomery that allowed Virginia Foster the financial freedom to transform her vague liberal inclinations into activism. Her husband, an introspective, bookish scholar, was a graduate of the University of Alabama and a Rhodes scholar who earned his law degree from England's Oxford University in 1922. The Durrs suited each other perfectly; everything Clifford did was in the cause of civil liberties, while Virginia focused her energies primarily on civil rights. Their work was complementary, but their methods differed: Clifford Durr armed himself with torts and laws in his battle for change, while Virginia Foster Durr opted for more direct political action. Clifford Durr "made a distinction between civil rights and civil liberties," wrote his young African-American protégé, Fred Gray, in his memoir, *Bus Ride to Justice*. "He believed that the rights of African American people had to be preserved and protected, not because they were African American, but because the denial of liberties to one group of Americans was an open invitation to undermine the entire body of civil law upon which this country is founded."

Everybody who was anybody in the nation's capital during the Great Depression knew the Durrs. They were champions of the underdog who saw no reason not to frequent Washington, D.C.'s tony Metropolitan and Chevy Chase Clubs. The couple were extremely well connected: Virginia's sister, Josephine, was married to Hugo Black, who was elected U.S. senator from Alabama in 1926 and appointed to the Supreme Court in 1937; Lyndon and Lady Bird Johnson of Texas were dear friends. Clifford Durr, at first distrustful of big government, served as assistant counsel for the Reconstruction Finance Corporation from 1933 to 1941, providing financial aid to railroads, corporations, and banks. The experience transformed him into a loyal FDR foot soldier. Later he was named to the Federal Communications Commission, where his tenure from 1941 to 1948 brought the Durrs into contact with many radio personalities and Hollywood stars.

While her husband was the dutiful bureaucrat, engrossed in writing his legal briefs and economic-forecast reports, the vivacious Virginia Foster Durr was more a cross between Jane

Addams and Zelda Fitzgerald. Despite her antebellum accent, Virginia Foster's blood boiled at southern bigotry. Even in her old age she made a point of telling reporters how she "hated" such "nasty polecats" as segregationists George Wallace and James Eastland, her "deep contempt" for whom she would take to her grave. She became a partner of Mary McLeod Bethune's in her quest to abolish the poll tax and an acolyte of Eleanor Roosevelt's through her work for the Women's Division of the Democratic National Committee. She also chaired Henry Wallace's 1948 presidential campaign in Virginia while at the same time running for the U.S. Senate herself as a Progressive Party candidate.

But 1948 proved to be a bad year for the Durrs. Clifford refused reappointment to the FCC because of his objections to President Harry Truman's "loyalty oath" program for the executive branch, which he saw as an unconstitutional infringement on the liberties of civil servants. He became an ardent legal defender of the First Amendment rights of Communists, socialists, and radicals of every other stripe, as well as an armchair opponent of Jim Crow laws. A believer in the United Nations—and even in the "One World" movement—Durr soon found himself a target of J. Edgar Hoover's FBI, which monitored his activities as if he were a spy. By 1950, in fact, Clifford Durr's left-leaning philosophy had led Senator Styles Bridges of Maryland to excoriate him as a Communist sympathizer on the floor of the U.S. Senate.

It saddened the Durrs that so many hard-core New Dealers—including Arthur Schlesinger, Jr., Walter Reuther, and Hubert Humphrey—were abandoning social reform in favor of the anti-Communist activities of groups like Americans for Democratic Action. With the Red Scare going full throttle, the Durrs left Washington, D.C., for Denver, where Clifford Durr served as counsel for the National Farmers Union in 1951—only to be fired later that year after his wife signed a petition critical of the Korean War.

Social casualties of the cold war and nearly broke as a result, the Durrs returned to Montgomery to live with Clifford's mother in the spring of 1951; three years later, the couple moved to a house apartment at 2 Felder Avenue in the Cloverdale section of town. Although Clifford Durr had a small inheritance, the family had three children to raise and a fourth away at graduate school, and they had a hard time making ends meet. Together the couple established the Durr law firm, with Virginia Foster Durr serving as secretary, and began retaining black clients, many with civil-liberties complaints. White Montgomerians for the most part shunned them. The Durrs had become, as historian Taylor Branch described them, "threadbare patricians," exiles in their own home state.

And controversy continued to swirl around the couple. In 1954, Virginia Durr was subpoenaed to appear at special Senate Internal Security Subcommittee hearings in New Orleans, presided over by Democratic senator James Eastland of Mississippi, on McCarthyist charges of having Communist ties. "The idea of Jim Eastland, just as common as pig tracks as they used to say, trying to call me to account—it made me so angry my adrenaline began to rise," Virginia Foster Durr wrote in her autobiography, *Outside the Magic Circle*. "I was just mad as hops." When Eastland began attacking the Highlander Folk School of Tennessee—a training ground for labor and civil rights activists run by Myles Horton—as a bastion of Communist recruiting efforts, Clifford Durr grew edgy. But when U.S. government informer Paul Crouch charged his wife with being a Communist spy, Clifford snapped, lunging at the redbaiter, challenging him to a fistfight, all in front of the television cameras. A photograph of him being restrained by security guards made the front page of the *New York Times*.

Southerners understood that the Crouch-Eastland attacks on the Durrs were actually aimed at the U.S. Supreme Court and especially at Virginia Foster Durr's brother-in-law, Justice Hugo Black, in retribution for his decision to support the *Brown* decision. In a classic showdown, however, Virginia Foster Durr verbally humiliated Eastland in the New Orleans federal court. The couple handled the ordeal well; however, the taint of being called before the Internal Security Subcommittee remained. With Clifford Durr in ill health after suffering a mild heart attack in New Orleans, the couple returned to Montgomery, overnight heroes in the black community but dumped by their few remaining white clients. When it came to the Durrs, the color lines were clearly drawn; while the New Orleans case had been pending, in fact, Virginia Durr had received a telegram from the all-black Women's Political Council (WPC), offering its members prayers of support. Many of those club members were teachers at Alabama State University, civil rights activists like Jo Ann Robinson, Irene West, and Mary Fair Burks, who would help launch the Montgomery bus boycott the following year. Montgomery's black leadership trusted the Durrs and rejoiced with them at the *Brown* decision, which for the first time since Reconstruction had put the federal government on the side of the blossoming civil rights movement.

It was just four days after *Brown v. Board of Education* that the events that would eventually escalate into the Montgomery boycott were set in motion. On May 21, 1954, Jo Ann Robinson, a forty-eight-year-old professor of English at Alabama State University, known for her liberal activism and serious scholarship, wrote a frank letter to Mayor W. A. "Tacky" Gayle threatening him with a bus boycott if the system's treatment of African Americans did not improve. "Please consider this plea, and if possible, act favorably upon it," Robinson concluded her letter. "For even now plans are being made to ride less, or not at all, on our buses." This was no idle threat: as head of the local Women's Political Council, founded in 1946 in response to the League of Women Voters' refusal to integrate, Robinson knew how to mobilize support. Bus integration had been her top priority ever since she had been verbally abused by a driver at Christmastime of 1949 and forced to slink away "like a dog," as she put it. In the wake of the *Brown* decision, desegregating Montgomery's buses had become Robinson's crusade. While her letter to Mayor Gayle was polite in pointing out that other Alabama cities, such as Mobile, had instituted a more liberal front-to-back seating policy for blacks with no trouble, Robinson's message was also threatening, a warning to the white power structure that blacks were mobilizing to end Jim Crow, and soon.

It was during this defiantly post-*Brown* period that E. D. Nixon—who, along with former Alabama State football coach Rufus Lewis, had repeatedly complained to Montgomery's city commissioners about the mistreatment of blacks on the bus lines—introduced the Durrs to his former secretary, Rosa Parks. Little did any of them know how the relationship would evolve when Virginia Durr discovered that Parks was an accomplished seamstress and hired her on the spot to alter the dresses that the Durrs' eldest daughter, Ann, had handed down to her three younger siblings. "After that I sewed anything she needed done," Parks remembered. "I used to be embarrassed at the amount she'd charge to make a dress," Virginia Durr recalled. "She'd charge, say, three dollars, which was absurd. I'd have to just beat her down to charge twice as much, which was still very little." As the two women became friends, Virginia Durr grew worried about Parks's "strained circumstances"—her husband, Raymond, was often sick and not making much money at the Atlas Barber Shop, while Rosa had to care for her mother and work numerous part-time jobs just to keep the family fed. Virginia Durr considered Rosa Parks "one of the greatest" individuals she ever encountered, "the epitome of what you'd call the southern lady."

The ramshackle rooming house that the Durrs rented, with its ten Greek Revival columns standing imposingly around the veranda, was slowly becoming a sort of wayward salon for civil libertarians. In 1951 the Parks family had moved out of Centennial Hill and were now living in the Cleveland Courts housing project, in a cubbyhole of an apartment about two miles away. Virginia Durr and Rosa Parks spent many hours together on the Durrs' front-porch swing, watching the mockingbirds divebomb squirrels and discussing everything—from Ella Fitzgerald's vocal range to Jackie Robinson's batting average to the injustices in American society. By no means rich but worldly by virtue of education and experience, Virginia Foster Durr became a mentor to Rosa Parks, lending her books and including her in integrated women's prayer groups at the Durr home—a practice that ended when the white participants' husbands began decrying their wives' behavior in various church meetings.

Their friendship blossomed, yet Rosa Parks remained deferential to her employer, calling Virginia "Mrs. Durr" despite the older woman's constant entreaties that she use her first name. "I couldn't call her Rosa until she could call me Virginia," Durr wrote in *Outside the Magic Circle*. "And that took twenty-odd years." The stereotype of a black seamstress working for a white family was shattered at the Durr household—outside of family, Virginia Durr was one of the closest female friends Rosa Parks ever had in Montgomery. "She [Rosa Parks] is very quiet, determined, brave, and frugal, not [at] all sophisticated and very churchgoing and orthodox in most of her thinking," Virginia Durr wrote journalist Jessica Mitford about her new friend. "But thoroughly good and brave, and the people here have the highest respect for her. When she feels at ease and gets relaxed, she can show a delightful sense of humor, but it is not often."

A main topic of conversation among Nixon, the Durrs, Parks, and the WPC was the possibility of a bus boycott. With *Brown* on their minds and Jo Ann Robinson ready to mobilize the charge to city hall, the timing seemed right. At a meeting on February 23, 1954, at the Ben Moore Hotel, African-American business leaders told city officials that segregated bus seating was their number one grievance. It was unacceptable, the blacks argued, to be verbally abused and treated as lesser citizens when they constituted 75 percent of all the bus riders. As Jo Ann Robinson explained in her memoir, *The Montgomery Bus Boycott and the Women Who Started It*, working African-American women like Rosa Parks were the most incensed by the unfair bus system because they were most dependent on it to get to work. Yet most of Montgomery's black community leaders, including its church ministers, were afraid that a boycott would fail—that after a few days of walking to work, tired feet would win out over good intentions. While these discussions were going on, however, an incident occurred that jarred all sides into action.

Claudette Colvin, a fifteen-year-old junior at Booker T. Washington High School, had boarded the Highland Gardens bus on the afternoon of March 2, 1955, in front of the Dexter Avenue Baptist Church, where twenty-six-year-old Dr. Martin Luther King, Jr., was minister. No whites were on the bus when Claudette sat down in a middle seat, munching on a candy bar, and stared out the window. When the bus reached Court Square, however, whites began boarding. The driver, Robert W. Cleere, pointed to four African-American women, one of them Colvin, and demanded that they give up their seats. Under duress the three other women finally moved, but Colvin—fresh from writing a school paper denouncing the law that prohibited blacks from trying on clothes in white department stores on the grounds that they would "smell or grease up" the merchandise—held out. "Older black people were always respectful to white people," Colvin later recalled. "But the younger blacks began to rebel." The police arrived, knocked Colvin's books from her arms, grabbed her wrists, and physically removed her from the bus. "I kept saying, 'He has no right . . . this is my constitutional right . . . you have no right to do this!' " Colvin later testified in *Browder v. Gayle*. "And I just kept blabbing things out, and I never stopped. That was worse than stealing, you know, talking back to a white person." Worried that she might run away, the police handcuffed Colvin despite her hysterical screams, took her to the station, and charged the minor with assault, disorderly conduct, and violating the segregation law.

Word of the arrest swept through Montgomery's African-American community. It seemed that this was the ideal legal test case that Nixon and Robinson had been waiting for. Claudette Colvin had been active in the NAACP Youth Council, which met Thursday evenings in the tiny sanctuary of the Trinity Lutheran Church, where her adviser was none other than Rosa Parks, who had taught her pupils never to lose their dignity. As the girl told her version of the arrest to the Durrs, Nixon, and Robinson, she noted that "Mrs. Parks said always do what is right"—and that's what she did. It turned out that Colvin's great-grandfather, Gus Vaughn, had lived in Pine Level and that as a girl Rosa McCauley used to play with Claudette's mother, so the two women had an even closer connection. "His great-granddaughter must have inherited his sense of pride," Parks explained. "I took a particular interest in the girl and her case." Also underlying Colvin's civil disobedience—and Rosa's sympathy for her—was the arrest and conviction of Jeremiah Reeves, a Booker T. Washington High School classmate who had been charged with raping a white woman and placed on death row. Neither woman could forgive the framing of this teenager, a drummer in the school band. "I was in the ninth grade when it happened," Colvin said in 1993. "And that anger is still in me from seeing him being held as a minor until he came of age."

Poised for legal action on Colvin's behalf, Clifford Durr got in touch with Fred Gray, an ambitious twenty-four-year-old black attorney fresh out of Case Western University Law

School, to represent her. The goal was to negotiate a new seating arrangement for Montgomery's buses along the lines of the Mobile system, with blacks filling the seats from the back, whites from the front, and mingling in the erstwhile no-man's-land in the middle. A petition to this effect was sent to bus-company officials and city officials. There was no call to end segregation on the buses outright, and a troubled Rosa Parks refused to join Gray, Robinson, and Nixon in presenting the petition, considering it demeaning; as she told them, ever since that "mean-spirited driver" had thrown her off his bus in 1943, she had promised herself never to ask hostile whites for favors. Gray sympathized, and told Parks privately that his ultimate goal was "to destroy everything segregated."

To the surprise of many blacks, Police and Fire Commissioner David Birmingham—a well-intentioned white progressive who, in the spring of 1954, had hired four African-American police officers—agreed to the petition's compromise plan; but the bus company's lawyer rejected any deal. Then, on May 6, Judge Eugene Carter cleverly dismissed the segregation charge, nullifying the plan to take Colvin's case to a federal court on constitutional grounds. Also dismissed, as a sign of goodwill toward the black community, was the disorderly-conduct charge. Only the assault charge remained. To put the matter to rest, the judge announced that as a juvenile, all Colvin had to do was plead guilty, pay a small fine, and go back to high school none the worse for wear.

Parks, meanwhile, consoled the confused Claudette and began setting up a legal defense fund for her. It bothered some that there was an unruly, tomboy quality to Colvin, including a propensity for curse words and immature outbursts; but it was only when Nixon found out that Colvin was several months pregnant that the drive to boycott buses and press a legal case against Montgomery's City Lines began to lose momentum. The conservative blacks who attended the city's elite Baptist churches found it difficult to go to the mat for an unmarried, pregnant teenager with bad manners. "If the white press got ahold of that information, they would have [had] a field day," Parks recalled. "They'd call her a bad girl, and her case wouldn't have a chance. So the decision was made to wait until we had a plaintiff who was more upstanding before we went ahead and invested any more time, effort, and money."

Although Claudette Colvin's case ended with a whimper—no bus boycott materialized, and the court found her guilty and forced her parents to pay a fine—it proved a good dress rehearsal for the real drama shortly to come. The *Atlanta Constitution* put a bold headline over a story that spring about how one Sarah Mae Flemming had sued the city bus line of Columbia, South Carolina, for having enforced segregation laws against her as an African American. The U.S. Court of Appeals for the Fourth Circuit ruled that July that segregated bus seating was unconstitutional. Nixon, Robinson, and Parks now realized that if they could find the right plaintiff, they could desegregate Montgomery's buses. The question arose at the NAACP meetings where Rosa Parks often kept the minutes: Who?

It was in this tense atmosphere that Rosa Parks was offered an educational opportunity she couldn't resist: Virginia Durr had asked her if she would like to attend a training workshop at the Highlander Folk School in Monteagle, Tennessee, to discuss "Radical Desegregation: Implementing the Supreme Court Decision." Located on two hundred acres in the scenic Appalachian Mountains west of Chattanooga, since 1932 the Highlander Folk School had functioned as an integrated forum for addressing issues related to workers' rights and race relations. Its half dozen scattered buildings— including a big, red-framed summerhouse and the solid stone Harry Lasker Library, which contained more than three thousand volumes—were built around a man-made lake at the base of Bays Mountain. The surrounding Grundy County was known for its abysmal poverty, high infant-mortality rate, and white supremacist attitudes. Yet Highlander's founder, a local Cumberland Plateau boy named Myles Horton, was a tireless promoter of the "Social Gospel," a teacher and CIO labor organizer whose simple philosophy was that people are not powerless. A onetime student of theologian Reinhold Niebuhr's at the Union Theological Seminary, Horton patterned his Appalachian school on Jane Addams's Hull House and John Dewey's beliefs in learning by doing. Horton garnered support for his rural training center from the likes of First Lady Eleanor Roosevelt, Georgia novelist Erskine Caldwell, socialist politician Norman Thomas, and modernist Baptist minister Harry Emerson Fosdick. Even Horton's foes—and there were many—conceded that he was a force of nature.

Operating under the banners "Racial Democracy" and "An Economically Just Society," the Highlander Folk School has earned an exalted place in civil rights lore for having trained future activists such as Marion Barry, Jr., James Bevel, Julian Bond, Martin Luther King, Jr., John Lewis, and Diane Nash. As the journalist David Halberstam succinctly noted in his 1998 civil rights history, *The Children*, "A series of charges, some bogus, some reflecting the prejudice of the time, were leveled at it: Highlander was holding integrated classes and integration was illegal in Tennessee." In fact, the theme song of the civil-rights movement—"We Shall Overcome"—grew out of the meetings at this unusual school in the Tennessee hill country; it was Myles Horton's wife, Zilphia, who, along with folk troubadours Guy Carawan and Pete Seeger, transformed the traditional hymn into the full-fledged anthem that by the late 1950s had been adopted by both SNCC and the Southern Christian Leadership Conference (SCLC).

In a 1981 interview with Bill Moyers on PBS, Myles Horton, then seventy-five, related how the KKK had harassed him, the FBI had investigated him, the House Committee on Un-American Activities had interrogated him, and the local police had raided his home. He saved the harshest vituperation, however, for the mine owners of Tracy City, six miles away from his school, who accused Highlander of bringing the CIO to Grundy County to help recruit employees to join the United Mine Workers union. An advocate of radical industrial unionism, Horton was deemed a Communist subversive by anti–New Dealers, who finally had him arrested for selling beer without a license. But Horton always roared back, ever more dedicated to using education as "an instrument to bring about a new social order." On one occasion when the local authorities padlocked Highlander's buildings, he just laughed. When asked why he was taking the closing of his school so lightly, Horton responded: "You cannot padlock an idea." As Moyers noted, there was an "indestructible" quality to Horton, who took every rebuff as an opportunity in his constant search for new students to empower. "At Highlander, anywhere you went everybody was equal," Horton told Moyers in 1981. "I always said we were too small and too poor to discriminate. We didn't have any facilities to discriminate—there was no way we could have done it even if we wanted to."

Rosa Parks's opportunity to attend the Highlander Folk School came about when Myles Horton telephoned Virginia Foster Durr to see if she knew a Montgomerian—preferably black—who might be interested in a two-week scholarship. Without hesitation Virginia Durr replied, "Rosa Parks." Once off the phone, she ventured to Cleveland Courts to tell her protégée about Highlander, to explain how the school was training a new generation of civil rights activists. Parks said she would indeed like to attend the summer workshop but unfortunately could not afford the fifteen dollars for a round-trip bus ticket to Chattanooga. So Virginia Durr, herself pressed for cash, called on the liberal white editor of the faltering *Southern Farmer* magazine, Aubrey Williams—former head of FDR's National Youth Administration and a friend of E. D. Nixon's—and procured the necessary funds from him. Virginia Durr said she also sent Parks luggage and a swimsuit to take to Highlander, which Parks disputed in *My Story*. "Rosa Parks is one of the proudest people I've ever known in my life," Durr responded in *Outside the Magic Circle*. "She hated to admit that she didn't have a suitcase or bathing suit or money. It was painful for her. She was a very proud woman, so all of this had to be accomplished with a great deal of tact, which I am not noted for."

In any case, with bus ticket in hand, Rosa Parks readied herself to be trained. "This is to say that I accept with sincere appreciation the scholarship for the Desegregation Workshop," Parks wrote to Mrs. Henry F. Shipherd, Highlander's executive secretary. "The registration card is enclosed. I am certainly most grateful to Mrs. Durr for recommending me to you. . . . The Highlander Folk School seems like a wonderful place. I am looking forward with eager anticipation to attending the workshop, hoping to make a contribution to the fulfillment of a complete freedom for all people." It is a testament to Parks's commitment to smashing Jim Crow that she would take a leave of absence from her job at the Montgomery Fair Department Store—the largest retail establishment in town, on Court Square—to spend two weeks learning new strategies for activism. What's more, she went over the objections of her irate husband, who considered the Tennessee school "suspect."

Upon arriving in Monteagle, the forty-two-year-old Parks at first felt self-conscious and apprehensive; she was inarticulate at the early roundtable discussions and overly formal toward her forty-seven classmates, who were calling each other "brother" and "sister." While she attended the sessions on voting rights and school desegregation and performed the assigned duties posted on the program's bulletin board, Parks declined to take part in the extracurricular activities at Highlander, such as volleyball, square dancing, and swimming. But after a few days she began to shine as she shared her horror stories from Montgomery, relating how her brother had been mistreated after World War II, telling about the ordeal of Claudette Colvin, and describing the field interviews she had done for the NAACP. While nobody looked to her as a budding leader, she clearly displayed the qualities of a loyal and committed foot soldier. "We forgot about what color anybody was," Parks recalled of her stint at Highlander. "I was forty-two years old, and it was one of the few times in my life up to that point when I did not feel any hostility from white people. I experienced people of different races and backgrounds meeting together in workshops and living together in peace and harmony. I felt that I could express myself honestly, without any repercussions or antagonistic attitudes from other people."

Buried deep in the Rosa Parks papers, housed at Wayne State University in Detroit, are her twenty-two pages of lecture notes taken at Highlander, written in a round female hand on yellow legal pads in pencil. They begin on July 26 for a session she calls "Memo on School Desegregation" and continue for three days' worth of seminars, including an "Action Guide" on how to use radio and newspapers to get the word out. At one juncture Rosa poses a question to herself: "To whom would *action* be taken toward in first step to integrate?" The answer she provided was "the churches."

Highlander proved a revelation to Rosa Parks, and not just because whites fried her bacon, scrambled her eggs, and served her coffee at breakfast. Once over her initial hesitation, she got caught up in the folksy camaraderie and found her sense of purpose redrawn in workshop discussions, singalongs, tea breaks, and idle chitchat. If Highlander was an example of a truly integrated society, then Parks had to admit that the future held promise. With morning dew blanketing the lovely panorama of deer grazing alongside herds of cattle as songbirds filled the sky, Highlander was a cool antithesis to steam-pressing other people's clothes at a downtown department store without air-conditioning in unbearable summer heat. For the first time in her life, Rosa Parks was being catered to instead of catering to others. She thrilled to hear stories about Thurgood Marshall's legal maneuvers and how the U.S. Fourth Circuit Court of Appeals in Richmond, Virginia, had ruled in *Fleming v. South Carolina Electric Gas Company* that intrastate bus segregation was unconstitutional. She found herself riveted by a wonderful seminar given by Dr. Fred Patterson, the president of the Tuskegee Institute, a scholar she had long admired.

But the greatest reward of attending Highlander for Parks was getting to know Septima Clark, a black activist from the Sea Islands of South Carolina who had studied with the legendary W. E. B. Du Bois at Atlanta University in 1937. Myles Horton had recruited the fifty-seven-year-old Clark, a veteran of numerous NAACP legal struggles, to serve as director of the school's workshops. Her time at Highlander, however, had not been easy. Once when Horton was away on a fund-raising trip, the local police raided the school, padlocked the buildings, and arrested Clark on false charges of drunkenness and communism—an outrage she wrote about with searing emotion in her memoir, *Echo in My Soul*. A born teacher, Clark served as a lightning rod for the integration of everything from bloodmobiles to public campgrounds.

A photograph taken that August at Highlander shows Clark and Parks relaxing together on lawn chairs in soft cotton dresses, their conversation apparently interrupted just long enough for the snapshot to be taken. From her pose Parks is clearly the eager student sitting at her wise elder's knee. What the picture shows is that for the first time Rosa Parks had found an African-American woman—besides her mother—to serve as her role model. "I am always very respectful and very much in awe of the presence of Septima Clark, because her life story makes the effort that I have made very minute," Parks later said, adding, "I only hope that there is a possible chance that some of her great courage and dignity and wisdom has rubbed off on me."

CHAPTER 6

The Bus Boycott

THE CAUSE OF WHITE SUPREMACY was upheld in the American South by law and tradition, and more chillingly, by violence and terror. So what was it that made a reserved, middle-aged black seamstress finally say enough is enough? And where did she get the physical and moral courage to say it so loud?

Sometimes it seemed as if Rosa Parks were two people: one, a traditionally submissive Negro laborer; the other, a modern African-American woman bold enough to demand her civil rights. "Rosa Parks was afraid for white people to know that she was as militant as she was," Septima Clark recalled. For after a week of riveting classes at Highlander, of reading Tolstoy's Nobel Peace Prize address, and of reacquaintance with Ella Baker, the obliging side of Parks melted away.

The Highlander Folk School—and Septima Clark in particular—had rubbed off on Rosa Parks. In the integrated pastoral idyll of Monteagle, the struggle against racism was recast in the philosophy of Gandhian nonviolence that was winning adherents across the embryonic national civil rights movement. Parks left Tennessee feeling empowered to be one of many African Americans who would no longer tolerate racist bullying and who would use the federal courts to dismantle American apartheid. "I gained the strength to persevere in my work for freedom," she said of her experiences at Highlander.

Parks remembers standing on a high bluff near her home overlooking a sharp bend in the Alabama River and sensing that the winds of the South had shifted—that Jim Crow was about to be blown to pieces. It felt suffocating to return to oppressive Montgomery, where the humidity soaked her checked blouses and fogged her wire-rimmed glasses while she swatted away the relentless flies. After the wide-open green grasslands of rural Appalachia, the rococo Monroe Avenue department store in which she now worked felt like a tomb. A feeling of unrest enveloped the city back when there was no air-conditioning to cool tempers in the muggy heat. With her eyes opened wider by Highlander, Parks saw more clearly than ever how routinely indignities were inflicted upon Montgomery's fifty thousand blacks, even ninety years after emancipation. When, she wondered, would her people abandon their go-along-to-get-along ways and stand together? When would justice prevail, as the New Testament promised? With a sullen heart Parks returned to the tailor shop in basement of the Montgomery Fair Department Store, where "you had to be smiling and polite no matter how rudely you were treated," she explained. And to get there she also had to return to the segregated buses that ran between Cleveland Courts and Court Square, always sitting behind the line marking the "colored section" and flinching every time she heard the driver call someone "nigger" or "boy" or "wench" or "coon," which was all too often.

Yet her hopes rose again that sultry summer on August 14, when she attended an NAACP meeting at the Metropolitan

United Methodist Church on Jefferson Davis Avenue. On that day, Rosa Parks had her first encounter with Dr. Martin Luther King, Jr., whose name would someday be one of the few from the civil rights movement more famous than her own. Thus, their first meeting, which has been left out of most biographies of King, is worthy of note. That evening, only thirty people showed up for King's NAACP address on the *Brown* decision—most of them women. Sitting up front were Rosa Parks and Johnnie Mae Carr, along with branch president Robert L. Matthews. Midway through King's speech, a mesmerized Carr elbowed her friend in the ribs and whispered, "He's something else." Parks responded, "He sure is!" According to Carr, their "jaws dropped" at King's mastery of his subject and at the cadences of his soaring deep voice. "I was very impressed by his eloquence," Parks remembered. "He looked like he might have been a student in college instead of a minister at a very prestigious church. . . . I thought he was well prepared to take a role of leadership in the community. But I didn't have any thought about how high he would go." A few days later, Parks wrote King inviting him to join the executive committee of the NAACP and to attend the next meeting to be held at the Pilgrim Health and Life Insurance Company, on Monroe Street. Unfortunately, he had a previous engagement.

But even King's upbeat lecture on civil rights progress couldn't numb her pain over the murder of Emmett Till that same August, just a few weeks after Parks's return to Montgomery. Till, a black fourteen-year-old from Chicago, was visiting his uncle in Leflore County, Mississippi, when he discovered that city street smarts were of no use in the Deep South. For the "crime" of saying, "Bye, baby," to a white woman, Carolyn Bryant, on a dare from some local boys as he left her country store in Money, Mississippi, Till was abducted and murdered by two white men—Bryant's husband and his brother-in-law, J. W. Milam—on August 13, 1955. A few days later, Till's mangled corpse was found in the Tallahatchie River with a crushed skull, an eye gouged out, a bullet in the brain, and a seventy-five-pound cotton-gin fan barbed-wired to the neck. Till's murder appalled the nation and raised cries for justice. As the NAACP executive secretary Roy Wilkins told the *New York Times*, "Mississippi has decided to maintain white supremacy by murdering children. The killer of the boy felt free to lynch because there is, in the entire state, no restraining influence of decency, not in the capital, among the daily newspapers, the clergy, not among any segment of the so-called lettered citizens." And Rosa Parks knew the same was true of Alabama.

Till's mother, Mamie Bradley, demanded an open-casket service for her son at Chicago's Ranier Funeral Home so that all could see what racial hatred had wrought. National and international reporters wrote scathingly about the segregationists of Mississippi. At a press conference after the funeral, Till's mother put her bitter grief in the form of a question: "Have you ever sent a loved son on vacation and had him returned in a pine box so horribly battered and waterlogged that someone needs to tell you this sickening sight is your son—lynched?"

Rosa Parks wept when she saw a grisly photograph of Till's body in *Jet* magazine, his face so bruised and distorted that the sight of it made her physically ill. But she had found another woman to place alongside Septima Clark in her pantheon of heroes: Mamie Bradley, who in the 1960s would become a close friend. By displaying her son's mutilated corpse, Till's thirty-three-year-old mother had galvanized black America into action. The name of Emmett Till became a rallying cry for justice and thus for change. A nationwide poll conducted by the *Cleveland Call and Post*, an African-American weekly newspaper, revealed that five of every six black radio preachers aired sermons on the fate of Emmett Till that month. Television coverage of the ensuing murder trial exposed the South's vicious racism to the entire nation. The image turned even uglier on September 23, 1955, when, after a five-day trial, an all-white jury in Sumner, Mississippi—having deliberated for just over an hour—found the suspects "not guilty" despite eyewitness identifications of them as Till's abductors. Most of America was horrified by Mississippi's twisted take on justice, and a wave of black outrage swept over the South, washing away any illusion that the present system could continue. With the murder of Emmett Till, a new era of defiance in the name of civil rights was at hand.

That September, central Alabama's home-grown racial troubles brought Parks face-to-face with another crusader for justice: Adam Clayton Powell, a Democratic congressman from New York who had journeyed South to express his outrage. The incident that drew Powell to Alabama began in Selma when twenty-nine blacks petitioned for immediate integration of the Dallas County schools. Prepared to go to any lengths to prevent desegregation, the local White Citizens Council applied political pressure to get sixteen of the offending blacks dismissed from their jobs. Selma's black leadership responded with a boycott of the Cloverleaf Dairy—the only one in town—for firing one of the petitioners. As the dairy's milk and cheese soured in crates unbought, one of the boycott leaders was abducted and beaten, further infuriating black Alabamans, who had been following the story on the front page of the *Montgomery Advertiser*.

The confrontational Powell, who was known for forcing his way into segregated restaurants and barbershops, responded to the Selma situation by traveling to Montgomery to make it absolutely clear to the White Citizens Council of Alabama that economic pressure—including boycotts— would continue. Powell stayed at E. D. Nixon's house on Clinton Avenue, and together the two mavericks plotted the movement's post-*Brown* integration strategies. Rosa Parks was present for many of their discussions and was thrilled by her proximity to the Harlem activist who proudly called himself "the first nigger in Congress," meaning the only fearless and strident black voice in 1950s Washington, D.C. "He was very funny and forceful in his approach," Parks recalled of Powell. "And he always called me 'honey.' "

The month after Powell's visit to Montgomery, yet another racial incident occurred on one of the city's buses. On October 21, a white woman on the Highland Avenue bus had asked the driver to force eighteen-year-old Mary Louise Smith to give up her seat. "I was sitting behind the sign that said 'for colored,' " Smith explained. "A white lady got on the bus, and she asked the driver to tell me to move out of my seat for her to sit there. He asked me to move three times, and I refused. So he got up and said he would call the cops. . . . I told him: 'I am not going to move anywhere. I got the privilege to sit here like anybody else.' " Because Smith had not violated the segregation law, the police instead arrested, jailed, and fined her for failing to obey an officer. The

NAACP considered making Mary Louise Smith's into a test case but backed off when Nixon found out that her family background did not lend itself to martyrdom: Her father was a drunkard. "She had to be deemed a bad risk," Nixon admitted later.

It was against this backdrop that Rosa Parks headed to work on December 1, 1955, on the Cleveland Avenue bus to Court Square. It was a typical prewinter morning in the Alabama capital, chilly and raw, topcoat weather. Outside the Montgomery Fair Department Store a Salvation Army Santa rang his bell for coins in front of window displays of toy trains and mannequins modeling reindeer sweaters. Every afternoon when school let out, hordes of children would invade the store to gawk at the giant Christmas tree draped with blinking lights, a mid-1950s electrical marvel. But Rosa Parks saw little of the holiday glitter down in the small tailor shop in the basement next to the huge steam presses, where the only hint of Yuletide cheer came from a sagging, water-stained banner reading "Merry Christmas and a Happy New Year."

Not that any of Montgomery Fair's lower-level employees had the time to let the faded decoration make them sad. The department store rang up nearly half of its sales between Thanksgiving and New Year's Day, which turned the tailor shop into a beehive of activity every December. But even on days spent frenetically hemming, ironing, and steam-pressing, Parks's mind was more with the NAACP than her workday duties. She was in the midst of organizing a workshop to be held at Alabama State University on December 3–4 and spent the morning during her coffee break telephoning H. Council Trenholm, president of the university, applying enough quiet persuasion to be granted the use of a classroom over the weekend. "I was also getting the notices in the mail for the election of officers of the senior branch of the NAACP, which would be [the] next week," Parks recalled. That afternoon, she lunched with Fred Gray, the lawyer who had defended Claudette Colvin and was serving as Clifford Durr's protégé at his law office above the Sears Auto Tire Store.

"When 1:00 P.M. came and the lunch hour ended, Mrs. Parks went back to her work as a seamstress," Gray would write in his civil rights memoir, *Bus Ride to Justice*. "I continued my work and left the office in the early afternoon for an out-of-town engagement."

Shortly after 5:00 P.M., Rosa Parks clocked out of work and walked the block to Court Square to wait for her bus home. It had been a hard day, and her body ached, from her feet swollen from the constant standing to her shoulders throbbing from the strain and her chronic bursitis. But the bus stand was packed, so Parks, disinclined to jockey for a rush-hour seat, crossed Dexter Avenue to do a little shopping at Lee's Cut-Rate Drug. She had decided to treat herself to a heating pad but found them too pricey. Instead, she bought some Christmas gifts, along with aspirin, toothpaste, and a few other sundries, and headed back to the bus stop wondering how her husband's day had been at the Maxwell Air Force Base Barber Shop and thinking about what her mother would cook for dinner.

It was in this late-day reverie that Rosa Parks dropped her dime in the box and boarded the yellow-olive city bus. She took an aisle seat in the racially neutral middle section, behind the movable sign which read "colored." She was not expecting any problems, as there were several empty spaces at the whites-only front of the bus. A black man was sitting next to her on her right and staring out the window; across the aisle sat two black women deep in conversation. At the next two stops enough white passengers got on to nearly fill up the front section. At the third stop, in front of the Empire Theater, a famous shrine to country-music fans as the stage where the legendary Hank Williams got his start, the last front seats were taken, with one man left standing.

The bus driver twisted around and locked his eyes on Rosa Parks. Her heart almost stopped when she saw it was James F. Blake, the bully who had put her off his bus twelve years earlier. She didn't know his name, but since that incident in 1943, she had never boarded a bus that Blake was driving. This day, however, she had absentmindedly stepped in. "Move y'all, I want those two seats," the driver barked on behalf of Jim Crow, which dictated that all four blacks in that row of the middle section would have to surrender their seats to accommodate the single white man, as no "colored" could be allowed to sit parallel with him. A stony silence fell over the bus as nobody moved. "Y'all better make it light on yourselves and let me have those seats," Blake sputtered, more impatiently than before. Quietly and in unison, the two black women sitting across from Parks rose and moved to the back. Her seatmate quickly followed suit, and she swung her legs to the side to let him out. Then Parks slid over to the window and gazed out at the Empire Theater marquee promoting *A Man Alone*, a new Western starring Ray Milland.

The next ten seconds seemed like an eternity to Rosa Parks. As Blake made his way toward her, all she could think about were her forebears, who, as Maya Angelou would put it, took the lash, the branding iron, and untold humiliations while only praying that their children would someday "flesh out" the dream of equality. But unlike the poet, it was not Africa in the days of the slave trade that Parks was thinking about; it was racist Alabama in the here and now. She shuddered with the memory of her grandfather back in Pine Level keeping watch for the KKK every night with a loaded shotgun in his lap, echoing abolitionist John Brown's exhortation: "Talk! Talk! Talk! That didn't free the slaves. . . . What is needed is action! Action!" So when Parks looked up at Blake, his hard, thoughtless scowl filled her with pity. She felt fearless, bold, and serene. "Are you going to stand up?" the driver demanded. Rosa Parks looked straight at him and said: "No." Flustered and not quite sure what to do, Blake retorted, "Well, I'm going to have you arrested." And Parks, still sitting next to the window, replied softly, "You may do that."

Her majestic use of "may" rather than "can" put Parks on the high ground, establishing her as a protester, not a victim. "When I made that decision," Parks stated later, "I knew I had the strength of my ancestors with me," and obviously their dignity as well. And her formal dignified "No," uttered on a suppertime bus in the cradle of the Confederacy as darkness fell, ignited the collective "no" of black history in America, a defiance as liberating as John Brown's on the gallows in Harpers Ferry.

The situation put Blake in a bind. This woman would, of course, have to be evicted from his bus. But should he do it himself, or should he call the police? Would it be better just to take her name and address and report her to the authorities later? Uncertain of what to do, he radioed his supervisor.

"I see it said as how I got up and swore at her and then went and called the police and told them to come get her," Blake told *Washington Post* reporter Paul Hendrickson in 1989 after years of remaining silent about the incident. "Well, I called the company first, just like I was supposed to do. Nobody ever wrote that. I got my supervisor on the line. He said, 'Did you warn her, Jim?' I said, 'I warned her.' And he said, and I remember it just like I'm standing here, 'Well, then, Jim, you do it. You got to exercise your powers and put her off, hear?' And that's just what I did."

Within minutes, Montgomery police officers F. B. Day and D. W. Mixon arrived and listened to Blake's account of what had transpired. Parks just watched as the three white men conferred on her fate, and realized what it would be: She would be fingerprinted and put in jail. The other passengers, black and white alike, began getting off the bus quietly but nervously, some with the self-possession to ask for transfers, others too anxious in the volatile situation. The blacks who remained on the bus sat in stunned, silent recognition that this time the authorities had picked the wrong woman to mess with. "It was like a mosque inside," one passenger recalled. "You could have heard a pin drop. It's as if we were all praying to Allah."

The two policemen then boarded the bus, less than thrilled at the prospect of arresting a prim, well-mannered, middle-aged woman on charges of violating the segregation code. When Officer Day asked Parks why she had refused to stand, she replied with a question that had no moral answer: "Why do you all push us around?" Day responded with a shrug and the only justification he could muster: "I don't know, but the law is the law, and you're under arrest." Then he picked up Parks's purse, Mixon gathered her shopping bags, and together they escorted her to their squad car. They did not handcuff Parks or mistreat her in any way. In fact, Parks saw them as two tired beat cops with no desire to waste their time and effort writing up reports for minor offenses.

At that point Parks was only in police custody, not officially arrested. For that a warrant would have to be sworn out and signed at city hall. On the way there Officer Day, more curious than angry, again asked Parks, "Why didn't you stand up when the driver spoke to you?" This time she said nothing. Calm had descended upon her; Parks had entrusted herself to the Lord's hands.

Just about everyone who hears the story of Rosa Parks asks the same question: Was her refusal to give up her seat premeditated? Did she intend to become the NAACP's test case against segregation? The answer to both is no. Rosa Parks did not wake up on the morning of December 1, 1955, primed for a showdown over civil rights with the local police. A lifetime's education in injustice—from her grandfather's nightly vigils to the murder of Emmitt Till—had strengthened her resolve to act when the time came. What arose in Parks that fateful evening was her belief in what Dr. Martin Luther King, Jr., often said: that "some of us must bear the burden of trying to save the soul of America." On her way home that night, Parks had no intention of making the headlines or history: She was thinking about relaxing for a rare moment, propping her feet up on the sofa, listening to a couple of Christmas carols, and preparing for that evening's NAACP Youth Council meeting. But when a white man tried to use an unfair system to undermine her dignity, Rosa Parks realized that it was *her burden* to stay put. "Just having paid for a seat and riding for only a couple blocks and then having to stand was too much," she told the Highlander Folk School's executive committee at a meeting a few months later. "These other persons had got on the bus after I did. It meant that I didn't have a right to do anything but get on the bus, give them my fare, and then be pushed wherever they wanted me. . . . There had to be a stopping place, and this seemed to have been the place for me to stop being pushed around and to find out what human rights I had, if any."

By the time her arrest was processed at Montgomery's city hall, Rosa Parks's spirit had hardened. She knew that the police were wrong, that she *had* sat in the "colored section," that she *had* obeyed the rules. Parched from the ordeal, she eyed a water fountain, and Officer Day gave her permission to take a drink. But Officer Mixon quickly stepped in. "No! You can't drink no water," he shouted. "It's for whites only. You have to wait till you get to the jail." It was the only time that Parks grew angry during her arrest—a grown man, a law enforcement officer no less, and presumably a Christian, was denying a tired, middle-aged woman a sip of water. She couldn't help but think of the Roman soldiers who had given Jesus only vinegar to drink on the road to Calvary.

Parks filled out the required forms and asked if she could make a telephone call to let her husband know where she was. Her request was denied. As the policemen escorted her from city hall to their squad car, she remembers chuckling to herself. Who would have thought that little Rosa Mc-Cauley—whose friends teased her for being such a Goody Two-shoes in her dainty white gloves—would ever become a convicted criminal, much less a subversive worthy of police apprehension, in the eyes of the state of Alabama?

The city jail on North Ripley Street was calm when Parks arrived, ready to accept her fate, whether a tongue-lashing, a beating, or even worse. After all, it had not been that long ago that a black man had been shot to death just for demanding his fare back when he got off a bus he had decided was too crowded to ride. Parks's fears were overblown, but her jail experience was hardly pleasant. She was fingerprinted and had her mug shots taken; her handbag was confiscated, and once again she was denied a drink of water. After she was processed, a female guard led Parks up a flight of stairs to the iron-barred cells on the second floor. A rank odor permeated the corridor, which was silent but for the clang of keys, the sound of their footfalls, and the racking cough of a sickly fellow prisoner. The guard put Parks in a dank, musty cell by herself, then walked away. Within seconds she returned, offering Parks the option of a larger cell with two other women. By this time indifferent to her accommodations, Parks chose the latter and once again asked to make a telephone call. Again her request was denied.

Parks recounts her brief stint in jail in My Story, a straightforward narrative that makes a valuable companion piece to Thoreau's essay on "Civil Disobedience" and King's "Letter from a Birmingham City Jail." She describes how one of her cellmates gave her some water from a tin cup and started talking. The woman had been incarcerated for almost two months for having defended herself by waving a hatchet at her boyfriend when he started beating her. As a result, the judicial system had her under lock and key with no way out, since her boyfriend, obviously, was not about to come to her rescue. Prevented from phoning her brother by the arbitrary dictates of the police and unable to make bail herself, she was a poor black woman alone in the world and facing a future as grim as her present. Hearing her cellmate's litany of woes made Parks realize how fortunate she was to have a husband like Raymond who would stick with her through thick and thin. But despite the differences in their situations, a bond was forged between the two women as they talked of the double burden of being black and female in 1950s America. The woman scribbled her brother's telephone number on a scrap of paper and gave it to Parks, who promised to call him if and when she got out.

After another hour or so, Parks was allowed to telephone home. Her mother answered. "I'm in jail," her daughter stated matter-of-factly. "See if Parks will come down here and get me out." Raymond Parks was on the line in a flash to make sure his wife was okay. She reassured him that the police were cordial and that she had not been beaten. "I'll be there in a few minutes," he told her, but she knew it would be longer than that, as they didn't own a car. "My husband was very upset," Parks recalled. "My mother was, too. After they found that I was okay—that I hadn't been physically manhandled—they felt better."

Word of Rosa Parks's arrest had already spread through Montgomery's black community. Another passenger on the bus that would go down in history had told Parks's friend Bertha Butler about the showdown with Blake. Butler had immediately contacted E. D. Nixon's wife, Arlet, with the shocking news that angelic Rosa Parks had been arrested. Arlet Nixon left a message for her husband at his office downtown, then paced around their Clinton Avenue home wondering what to do. She was relieved when he finally rang back, asking, "What's up?"

"You won't believe it," Arlet Nixon replied. "The police got Rosa. She's in jail, but nobody knows the extent of the charges or whether she's been beaten. You better get her out." All Nixon could manage in response was "Holy mother of God." He called the police station to find out what the charges were, but "they wouldn't talk with me because I was black," he remembered. "They couldn't have been ruder." So Nixon decided to seek the help of his friend Clifford Durr, a white lawyer the police would have to cooperate with.

"I asked Clifford if he would call the jail and find out why in hell they arrested Rosa Parks," Nixon recalled. Durr did so immediately, especially outraged that a friend was being denied her civil liberties. The officer he talked to told Durr that Rosa Parks had been booked for violating the city's segregation ordinance, with bail set at one hundred dollars. Their paying white clients having abandoned them, the Durrs were broke, so Nixon offered to post Parks's bond himself. But even so, he asked Durr to come to the jail with him for fear that corrupt police would try to take his money without releasing Parks. The Durrs found themselves heading to the city jail in E. D. Nixon's blue Plymouth to bail out their friend, all discussing the possibility of making this the NAACP's Jim Crow test case. They all agreed that the moment for action had arrived. "I waited for them while they made bail," Virginia Durr wrote later in *Outside the Magic Circle*. "Everything went very smoothly. They brought Mrs. Parks out from behind the bars. That was a terrible sight to see: this gentle, lovely, sweet woman, whom I knew and was so fond of, being brought down by a matron. She wasn't in handcuffs, but they had to unlock two or three doors that grated loudly."

What impressed Virginia Durr most about the moment was how tranquil Rosa Parks remained, the epitome of grace under pressure. As Nixon signed the bond papers, Raymond Parks came in, close to tears. He gave his wife a bear hug that swept her off her feet as her two-hour ordeal came to an end. The Durrs hopped into Nixon's Plymouth, and the trio followed Raymond Parks, driving a car hastily borrowed from a friend, back to Cleveland Courts. There they held a powwow over coffee to take stock of what had happened.

Nixon refrained from discussing legal strategies straight off, sensing that Rosa Parks wanted to return to normalcy— to change her clothes, eat dinner, and run her regular Thursday NAACP Youth Council meeting at the tiny Trinity Lutheran Church across the street. When Nixon accompanied her to the church, however, he used their time alone to lobby his friend to let her arrest become a civil-rights test case, taking care not to push too hard and to give Parks time to assess her options. This was not easy, for from the moment he had first heard A. Philip Randolph speak of civil rights in St. Louis, E. D. Nixon had been itching for a direct confrontation with "Mr. Charlie," as he called the white power establishment. He couldn't help but see it as a gift from God that Mr. Charlie had been fool enough to arrest Rosa Parks, but to his consternation, he sensed reluctance on the part of his intended heroine. Nixon asserted in an interview that he had to prod Parks into taking a public stand, a contention strongly disputed by Virginia Foster Durr. "Mr. Nixon remembers her as being extremely reluctant to do it, but I remember that it was her husband who was so reluctant," Durr recalled. "He kept saying, over and over again: 'Rosa, the white folks will kill you. Rosa, the white folks will kill you.' It was like a background chorus—to hear the poor man, who was as white as he could be himself—for a black man, saying, 'Rosa, the white folks will kill you.' I don't remember her being reluctant."

But Rosa Parks would not be rushed into a decision; she had to consider the potential impact of filing a lawsuit on her husband and mother, both of whom were aghast at the prospect of Rosa's becoming a public spectacle. For one thing, she was the family's principal breadwinner, and becoming the NAACP poster woman for desegregation was bound to get her fired from her job at Montgomery Fair. What's more, Parks's husband and mother had been warning her for years that working with E. D. Nixon and the NAACP would get her lynched from the tallest telephone pole in town someday. It was one thing to be arrested for an isolated bus incident; it was quite another, as historian Taylor Branch would put it in *Parting the Waters*, to "reenter that forbidden zone by choice."

Rosa Parks already knew, of course, that a court case would turn her into even more of an outcast in white Montgomery. Although unconcerned about her own physical safety, she also knew that any public position she took would cause dire trouble for her husband: the police would harass him, perhaps even frame him on some trumped-up charge. Her mother's health, meanwhile, was frail: Could she endure a long-drawn-out trial? Rosa Parks fretted over these dilemmas, but in her heart she never doubted what she had to do. As compelling as she found the Highlander School's teachings on Gandhi's philosophy of nonviolence, as attractive as those methods were proving to a growing number of black activists, including Martin Luther King, Jr., Rosa Parks's own philosophy came closer to the views of playwright Lorraine Hansberry: "Negroes must concern themselves with every single means of struggle: legal, illegal, passive, active, violent, and non-violent. They must harass, debate, petition . . . sit in, sing hymns . . . and shoot from their windows when racists come cruising through their communities." As a Christian, Parks's stance in defense of herself and her fellow blacks would always be tempered by mercy, even toward her tormentors. Indeed, she believed in the righteousness of turning one's cheek once or twice—but she also believed that the oppressed eventually had to fight back. As she saw it, the Holocaust should have taught everyone the futility of battling evil with passive resistance alone. In a revealing 1967 interview on file at Howard University, she said candidly, "I don't believe in gradualism or that whatever is to be done for the better should take forever to do."

Unaware how little need he had to beat around the bush, E. D. Nixon finally came to the point. "Mrs. Parks," he said, "with your permission, we can break down segregation on the bus[es] with your case." Replying with remarkable composure, Rosa Parks confirmed that she would challenge the constitutionality of the ordinance under which she had been arrested, to Nixon's jubilation. And thus did an ordinary, civic-minded woman give birth to the modern civil-rights movement.

Still, brainstorming in the Parks's living room as 9:00 P.M. approached, the Durrs, Nixon, and Rosa Parks turned to the practical questions involved in what they were planning: Who would finance the lawsuit? "Now, if you're going to fight this on a constitutional basis, you will have to get the NAACP to finance it, because it's going to cost you a fortune," Clifford Durr told Parks. "It'll have to go all the way up to the Supreme Court of the United States, and it's going to cost a lot of money." It didn't help matters that the Montgomery NAACP's coffers were essentially bare and that even the organization's state chapter lacked the financial resources to support a costly, and possibly protracted, legal battle.

It was at that point, late in the evening, that Clifford Durr mentioned the NAACP Legal Defense and Educational Fund, headed by Thurgood Marshall, who would win twenty-nine of the thirty-two major cases he argued for the NAACP and eventually be appointed to the U.S. Supreme Court in 1967. Fred Gray had close ties to Marshall's group, which Clifford was confident would take the case eagerly once they became acquainted with Parks's sterling character. By 11 P.M. a strategy was in place: Rosa Parks, with Gray serving as her attorney, would challenge Montgomery's bus-segregation ordinance on constitutional grounds, supported, if necessary, by the NAACP Legal Defense and Educational Fund. Clifford Durr would work with the national media and offer counsel as needed behind the scenes; he could not act as Parks's lawyer of record without forcing his brother-in-law, Justice Hugo Black, to recuse himself from the case to avoid conflict-of-interest charges.

The Cleveland Courts summit continued the tradition of the rebels who gathered in Philadelphia in 1776 to denounce King George III's "design to reduce them under absolute despotism." In December 1955, it was in the far more humble setting of Rosa and Raymond Parks's linoleum-floored living room that a group of Americans, with less than five hundred dollars among them, banded together to stand up for the principles of democracy by taking on the greatest failing in the United States' version. In his 1965 book *Who Speaks for the Negro?* author Robert Penn Warren reflected on why the Parks arrest was such a watershed moment. "An event is never single and isolated," he decided. "It is not a bright unit gleaming before the eye of God. It's a complex of various factors. It is hard to know where accident comes in. It is hard to know where necessity comes in." One thing Warren knew for certain, however: America was never the same after that fateful day.

Parks herself had no easy answer to the question of why that exact transformative moment: "I was determined to achieve the total freedom that our history lessons taught us we were entitled to, no matter what the sacrifice," she recalled. "When I declined to give up my seat, it was not that day, or bus, in particular. I just wanted to be free like everybody else. I did not want to be continually humiliated over something I had no control over: the color of my skin."

CHAPTER 7

Strength through Serenity

WHEN SHE GOT UP on the morning of December 2, 1955, a still-groggy Rosa Parks found herself news. A headline on page 9 of the *Montgomery Advertiser* read: "Negro Jailed for 'Overlooking' Bus Segregation," although the article gave only her place of employment, not her name. Embarrassed by the story nonetheless, and even more for now having a police record, Parks refused to dwell on her arrest. Instead, she searched for the paper her cellmate had given her in jail and dialed the phone number scrawled on it. She reached one of the woman's brothers and informed him that his troubled sister was locked up in the South Ripley Street Jail and desperate to get out. "He promised he would visit her," Parks related. "I prayed for her release. And within days she was out."

That pledge fulfilled, Parks got dressed for work as usual, but this Friday morning she telephoned her friend Felix Thomas, who operated a black taxi company—one of thirteen in Montgomery—and asked him for a lift. "I was not going to ride the bus anymore," she explained. At Montgomery Fair she encountered her boss, John Ball, who was shocked that his assistant had the temerity to show up for work after the events of the day before. Trying to make light of the uncomfortable situation, Parks smiled and asked Ball, "You don't think going to jail is going to keep me home, do you?"

She added, however, that she was curious why he hadn't called to see if she would be coming in. "Oh, I just thought that you'd be too nervous and upset, and I certainly didn't expect you to work today," he answered. Parks laughed. "I'm not at all nervous," she said, and turned to the day's garment list.

But the cordiality was short-lived. An hour later, the tailor-department supervisor came into the basement shop and glared at Parks without so much as his customary "Howyadoing?" Agitation was written all over the supervisor's face—the last thing Montgomery Fair needed was to be drawn into another high-profile public dispute with Negroes. Back in 1946 the Montgomery NAACP, while Parks was its secretary, had cooperated with a local citizens' committee in pressing the department store to rehire four elevator operators, black women who had resigned in protest of their employer's plan to force them to pull double duty, to do their work as well as that of the store porters, whom Montgomery Fair wanted to fire. Anxious to discredit the protest and the NAACP, Montgomery Fair kept the porters on staff and hired whites to take the black women's places. The last thing the store wanted now, at the height of the Christmas shopping season, was to have a "radical Negress" on its staff making antiwhite headlines with "Montgomery Fair" in them. The moment she saw her supervisor's face, Parks knew she would lose her job.

Meanwhile, a reporter from the *Montgomery Advertiser* was calling the store asking for a Mrs. Rosa Smith, the black woman who ran its Otis elevator, to inquire about her arrest in front of the Empire Theater. Parks took full advantage of the mistaken identity and avoided the local press all that day, as she did not yet know precisely what she wanted to say in public. This was hardly the case with E. D. Nixon, who in the coming weeks would boast about Parks to the press and anybody else who would listen. "My God, look what segregation had put in my hands," he exclaimed. "The perfect plaintiff." By all accounts Nixon was behaving like a father whose daughter had just won the Nobel Prize. The night before, after leaving the Parkses' apartment, Nixon—who had to leave town Friday morning on his Pullman run from Atlanta to New York and back—grabbed his tape recorder and paced around his kitchen rattling off the list of people he needed to call. At the top was attorney Fred Gray, who had just gotten home from an engagement out of town. After being thoroughly briefed by Nixon, Gray went into action, first telephoning Parks to hear her account and to offer his legal services at no cost. Next he called Jo Ann Robinson, the professor who headed the Woman's Political Council, made up of nearly three hundred of Montgomery's most active integrationists.

It was 11:30 P.M., and Robinson was sitting alone in her house when she was jolted by the jangle of her telephone so late at night. "Fred Gray and his wife, Bernice, were good friends of mine and we talked often," Robinson wrote in her memoir, *The Montgomery Bus Boycott and the Women Who Started It*. "Tonight his voice on the phone was very short and to the point. Fred was shocked by the news of Mrs. Parks's arrest. I informed him that I already was thinking that the WPC should distribute thousands of notices calling for all bus riders to say off the buses on Monday, the day of Mrs. Parks's trial." An eager Gray asked: "Are you ready?" Without pause Robinson assured him that the WPC was as prepared for the action as a SWAT team on alert. Unafraid of confrontation, Robinson sensed that Parks's arrest was the opportunity she had been waiting for. After consulting next with E. D. Nixon, she scrawled on the back of an envelope: "The Women's Political Council will not wait for Mrs. Parks to consent to call for a boycott of city buses. On Friday, December 2, 1995, the women of Montgomery will call for a boycott to take place on Monday, December 5."

Historian David Garrow, author of the 1987 Pulitzer Prize—winning *Bearing the Cross: Martin Luther King, Jr., and the Southern Christian Leadership Conference*, and Professor J. Mills Thornton III of the University of Michigan deserve the credit for making sure Jo Ann Robinson's place in history is not forgotten. More than any other individual, including Gray and even Parks herself, it was Robinson who organized the Montgomery bus boycott. After talking with Gray, Robinson headed to the Alabama State University campus at midnight under the pretext of having to grade exams. With the help of two female students and a business professor with access to a mimeograph machine, Robinson put together a 218-word, one-page boycott flyer to be distributed throughout black Montgomery the next morning. "Another Negro woman has been arrested and thrown into jail because she refused to get up out of her seat on the bus and give it to a white person," the manifesto began, referring to the failed Claudette Colvin case in March 1955. "If we do not do something to stop these arrests, they will continue," the leaflet went on. "The next time it may be you, or your daughter, or mother. This woman's case will come up on Monday. We are, therefore, asking every Negro to stay off the buses Monday in protest of the arrest and trial. Don't ride the buses to work, to town, to school, or anywhere on Monday." Robinson's call to action ended with an exhortation to black citizens to walk, taxi, or stay home come Monday—to do anything but board a Montgomery City Lines bus. After this unexceptional handbill was duplicated onto paper, cut in thirds, bundled by Jo Ann Robinson at 4:00 A.M., and distributed a few hours later to thirty-five hundred of Montgomery Alabama's homes, schools, and churches, America was never the same again.

At 3:00 A.M. that Friday morning, Robinson had telephoned Nixon, her fears of waking him immediately dispelled by the vigor in his voice. She told him of the mimeographed boycott declaration and how her students had carved up delivery routes to blanket black Montgomery with them by sunrise. They planned to distribute flyers to every black school, for example, so the children would take them home to their parents. Nixon told Robinson that he was going to assemble Montgomery's black leaders that afternoon for a meeting to organize both Parks's legal defense and the city bus boycott. As Martin Luther King, Jr., later noted, it was the combined efforts of Jo Ann Robinson and E. D. Nixon that brought Montgomery's historic protest to fruition.

All of this frenzied activity took place while Rosa Parks slept. At 5:00 A.M., Nixon thought it no longer too early to begin informing the city's black leaders of the game plan. His first call was to his own minister, Ralph David Abernathy, pastor of the First Baptist Church, in 1955 the oldest and largest black Baptist institution in Montgomery. When First Baptist's original wooden church burned down, in the 1880s, then pastor Andrew Stokes had exhorted his flock to bring one brick to the site each day to build a new one, which thus earned the nickname "Brick-a-Day Church." Now, with the bravely outspoken Abernathy as pastor and a facility so enormous some called it the Hollywood Bowl, First Baptist had become the Grand Central Station of civil rights preaching.

Abernathy's autobiography, *And the Walls Came Tumbling Down*—controversial for its unfortunate jealous criticism of Martin Luther King, Jr.—outlines the chronology of his life. Born on a farm in Linden, Alabama, one of twelve children, Abernathy served in the army, studied theology at a Baptist academy, and then moved to Montgomery to attend Alabama State College, from which he received his B.A. degree in 1950. A respectable orator, he became pastor of First Baptist in 1952, after which he moved the church parsonage to Centennial Hill and married Juanita Odessa Jones. Abernathy had long been audacious in his determination to abolish racial segregation. As Virginia Durr once noted, he was "not scared of hell or high water."

E. D. Nixon figured that Montgomery's black ministers could do more to mobilize support for the bus boycott than anyone else—and that mountains could be moved with the support of the twenty-nine-year-old Reverend Abernathy, who was secretary of the Baptist Ministers Alliance, on his side. Abernathy promised to do everything he could to get the city's other influential black pastors to attend a meeting that evening at Dr. Martin Luther King, Jr.'s Dexter Avenue Baptist Church, centrally located just a stone's throw away from the state capitol. Abernathy also suggested that Nixon contact two people: the Reverend H. H. Hubbard, the aged president of the Baptist Ministers Alliance, and Abernathy's best friend, King, whose church basement they would need.

To Nixon's surprise, King proved cautious and did not

jump on the boycott bandwagon right away, hedging even on endorsing it. "Brother Nixon," King said, "let me think about it and you call me back." Nixon couldn't help but wonder: Was King a jellyfish? Or was he looking out for his own political future? Those worries became irrelevant within minutes when Abernathy telephoned King, gave him the hard sell, and quickly convinced him to join the ranks. The chore of calling all the other black ministers was thus shared by King and Abernathy, while Nixon headed to work at Union Station to catch his Atlanta-bound train, pushing the boycott until his last minute in town. In fact, Nixon met with Joe Azbell, city editor of the *Montgomery Advertiser*, on the station platform to feed him the "hottest story you've ever written." Azbell—a smart, progressive white reporter—thus heard the life story of Rosa Parks, a dignified, reserved, and respected mulatto woman of impeccable moral character. Then Nixon informed him of the planned Monday bus boycott and of how the city's black ministers were prepared to lead the charge in Montgomery just as the Reverend T. J. Jemison had in Baton Rouge two and a half years before. Nixon made it juicy, knowing if Azbell wrote a story anticipating the boycott, the word would reach virtually every member of the local black community.

All of these frantic maneuvers were well along by the time Parks took her lunch break and headed over to Fred Gray's law office just blocks away. Brown bag in hand, she was shocked by the bustle she found there—telephones ringing, streams of people quick-stepping every which way, a radio blaring. It was like a big-city newsroom close to deadline, with Fred Gray playing editor in chief. "*Jet* magazine was there," Parks recalled. "Fred was moving about, talking with me. The *Jet* people started taking my picture and asking questions." Her replies were noble and honest. And from that moment on Rosa Parks would never again be just a hardworking Alabama seamstress but the woman whose staying seated shook the world into a better state. She had become a symbol of courage, a darling of the liberal press, and one of the most famous women in history.

After work Parks returned to her Cleveland Courts apartment for a spaghetti dinner cooked by Raymond before heading to Dexter Avenue Baptist Church to speak to the black leaders assembled by Abernathy and King. While she was eating, the telephone rang; it was her friend the Reverend Robert S. Graetz, a baby-faced, idealistic twenty-seven-year-old minister from West Virginia who had recently moved to Montgomery to serve as pastor of the Trinity Lutheran Church, where Rosa held her NAACP Youth Council meetings. After exchanging greetings, Graetz said, "I just heard that someone was arrested on one of the buses Thursday," to which Parks replied, "That's right, Pastor Graetz." He added, "And that we're supposed to boycott the buses on Monday to protest," and again she responded, "That's right, Pastor Graetz." Then he asked, "Do you know anything about it?" And Parks said quietly, "Yes, Pastor Graetz." Still unsatisfied, he continued: "Do you know who was arrested?" Once again he received a polite "Yes, Pastor Graetz." Finally, exasperated by this game of Twenty Questions, Graetz blurted out, "Well, who was it?" After a long pause, Parks replied: "It was me, Pastor Graetz." He immediately rushed over to Cleveland Courts to hear all the details.

There was nothing coy in Parks's exchange with Graetz, who would remain a lifelong friend. Her authentic self-deprecation was just Parks being herself as always. Never the prima donna, her genuine dignity made her shine even in the erudite, college-educated company of King, Nixon, Gray, and Abernathy. Parks shared their nobility and passion but added to them the profoundest humility, gentleness, and decency. She may have lacked her cohorts' vocabulary and worldliness, but part of her lasting appeal is that nobody ever had a bad word to say about her. And she returned the favor, as her friendships with Graetz, the Durrs, and other whites showed: Parks harbored no race bias or any other uncharitable suspicions in her open mind or in her truly good soul. It was these same qualities, of course, that made it impossible for her not to fight for what is right.

It was in the first flowering of this ethereal authority that Rosa Parks headed to Dexter Avenue Baptist Church that first Friday evening of December 1955. Earlier that day at Gray's law office, she had learned that Dr. King was helping to spearhead the bus boycott—reassuring news indeed. Although Parks was not close to King, since her first encounter with him at Metropolitan United Methodist Church, she had admired not only his gifts for preaching the gospel with authority and making everybody feel at ease but also his ability to laugh. She also liked the facts that he had graduated from Morehouse College and Crozer Theological Seminary, that his father was one of Atlanta's most respected black preachers, and that his beautiful wife, Coretta Scott King, was a musically talented Alabama "homegirl" from nearby Marion, only eighty-four miles away. When Dexter Avenue Baptist had installed King as the church's twentieth pastor on October 31, 1954, Parks deemed it a wise choice—not from any study of his résumé or analysis of his intellect but simply because he was only twenty-five and had already accomplished so much, she couldn't imagine what he might achieve in the future. At a time when African-American cultural heroes such as singer Paul Robeson and novelist Richard Wright were falling victim to McCarthyism, King appeared to Parks exactly what black America needed: a heart filled with Christian love for the downtrodden untainted by flashy opportunism or radical rhetoric. What's more, she sensed within his goodness a bullheaded resolve, not unlike her own, not to get gored by Mr. Charlie.

When Rosa Parks arrived that evening, the basement of Dexter Avenue Baptist was crowded with some fifty black leaders, nearly all with conflicting views and agendas. As Taylor Branch recounts in *Parting the Waters: America in the King Years, 1954–1963*, a "protracted and often disorderly argument" ensued over whether to follow E. D. Nixon's boycott plan. Parks's presence served to quiet the dissenting ranks. She stood up before these leading men of her community and gently explained to them her weariness with Jim Crow buses, the circumstances of her arrest, and the need for collective action in response to both. Gender was on her side with this crowd: With a touch of chauvinistic chivalry, many of the ministers did not want to be on record as abandoning a good Christian woman in need. Most of those assembled therefore embraced "Sister Rosa," promising to promote the one-day boycott in their Sunday sermons and to meet again Monday night to assess how the protest went. After most of the ministers left that night, Parks joined King, Abernathy, and a few others in drafting a new, shorter version of Jo Ann Robinson's handbill, adding the line "Come to a mass meeting Monday at 7:00 P.M. at the Holt Street Baptist Church, for further instruction."

Years later, Parks could still recall her delight when she woke up the following Sunday morning to find a copy of Jo Ann Robinson's handbill reprinted on the front page in the *Montgomery Advertiser*. The newspaper publicity meant that even nonchurchgoers would know about the boycott the next day. Yet Parks remained apprehensive. Would enough black Montgomerians actually walk to work to make an impact? Would the city's black-owned taxi companies charge African-American passengers only a dime and pick them up at bus stations, as promised? What if it rained on Monday, as the radio weatherman was predicting? Would other whites besides Reverend Graetz, the Durrs, and Aubrey Williams support the effort? What if violence broke out and people were killed? Would she be able to live with herself? Parks spent all day Sunday after church praying and pondering, but she knew that all she could do was wait and see.

And she liked what she saw at dawn on Monday: the Cleveland Avenue bus going past the projects virtually empty, a misty rain glazing the road. Over the weekend King had said that if 60 percent of Montgomery's blacks cooperated, the boycott could be deemed a success. In his book on the Montgomery bus boycott, *Stride Toward Freedom*, King recounted how he sat in his South Jackson Street kitchen that morning, waiting for the 6:00 A.M. bus to pass with the first signal of victory or failure. As he sipped his coffee, suddenly his wife cried, "Martin! Martin, come quickly!" He bolted to the living-room window and crowed: "Darling, it's empty!" That particular route carried more African Americans than any other in the city, but that morning, to King's delight, there was not a black face to be seen on the 6:00 A.M. bus. Unable to sit still, King jumped into his car and drove around eyeing other buses; they too, were devoid of blacks. "A miracle had taken place," King would write of the near-100 percent participation in the boycott. "The once dormant and quiescent Negro community was now fully awake."

That brisk and windy morning, Rosa and Raymond Parks swelled with pride as they headed to city hall for her 9:30 A.M. trial. Everywhere they looked, determined African Americans were walking to work or on errands, some carrying heavy tool belts or cumbersome bags of laundry. Excited youngsters ran after the empty buses, pointing at their uselessness and shouting, "No riders today!" Each bus passing through the city's black neighborhoods was accompanied on its route by two police motorcycle escorts, assigned by the city government to prevent imaginary "Negro goon squads" from intimidating passengers. But there were no African-American passengers to intimidate.

The unanimity of the black community's collective action baffled the police and disturbed the city's white power elites, who responded by whispering that Rosa Parks was a trained Communist or that the NAACP had "planted" her on James Blake's bus. The allegations were not without the appearance of merit, for two reasons: She *had* attended the radical Highlander Folk School and had been the secretary of the Montgomery NAACP. "So persistent and persuasive was this argument that it convinced many reporters from all over the country," King would later lament. "Later on, when I was having press conferences three times a week—in order to accommodate the reporters and journalists who came to

Montgomery from all over the world—the invariable first question was: 'Did the NAACP start the bus boycott?' " The accusation, as King knew, was false, but the suspicion never died away.

A crush of people choked the entrance to city hall, located at 103 North Perry Street, diagonally across from the Montgomery Fair store, when the Parkses arrived. The last time this block-long, two-story, redbrick edifice, fronted by six imposing Roman columns, had attracted such a crowd was in 1953, when Hank Williams died of heart failure and more than twenty thousand country-music fans held an open-casket funeral vigil in the Municipal Auditorium before the singer's burial at nearby Oakwood Annex Cemetery. There was a noticeable difference between these crowds at Montgomery's city hall two years apart: The throng that gathered to honor Williams had been almost exclusively white, while those who congregated for Parks's trial were almost all black.

Just about all five hundred of the African Americans who assembled on the steps of Montgomery's city hall that first day of the 1955 bus boycott shared one distinct impression: how elegant Rosa Parks looked in her long-sleeved black dress, with its starched white collar and cuffs, black velvet hat with faux pearls around the top, and straight dark gray coat. As she arrived on the scene, headed for the Recorders Court, where she would be tried, the crowd erupted into thunderous applause. "I was not especially nervous," Parks recalled. "I knew what I had to do. . . . You could hardly see the street for the crowds. Many members of the NAACP Youth Council were there, and they were all shouting their support."

One of those Youth Council members, Mary Frances, made the history books that December 5 by exclaiming, "Oh, she's so sweet. They've messed with the wrong one now," a cry immediately taken up by the assembled well-wishers and carried on. "They've messed with the wrong one now" would echo through the city for the next year as black Montgomerians walked, took taxis, or carpooled to work and school. The slogan served as a reminder that the woman who had inspired the boycott was the sort of soft-spoken martyr God would not abandon.

Flanked by the only two black lawyers in Montgomery, Fred Gray and Charles Langford, Rosa Parks marched into city hall, down a long, muted corridor, through a pair of swinging mahogany doors, and into a packed courtroom, all hundred of its segregated seats filled but for the few in the front row reserved for city staff. The defense team's strategy was simple: Parks would not testify on her own behalf but would sit and listen to the prosecution's witnesses, then plead "Not Guilty" to violating the city's segregation laws. The outcome of guilty, however, was a given, as the lower court judges—in this case one John B. Scott—were part of Montgomery's white power establishment and would never rule in favor of an African American who had broken a Jim Crow law. The whole judicial process was a charade. Parks and her legal advisers knew that if hers was to become the NAACP's test case, she would have to be convicted, and they would have to appeal the verdict first at the district-court level and then, if necessary, to a federal court.

The strategy worked, but the proceedings were not easy on Parks. The chief witness for the prosecution was James F. Blake, of the small town of Seman—ironically just a few miles south of Equality, Alabama. His hair slicked back and his tie too short, Blake looked unfazed at the prospect of what he knew was a preordained outcome. For the most part Blake's version of the incident in question comported with Parks's account, except for his false claim that there had been a vacant seat in the back of the bus. This crucial untruth was repeated by two white women prosecutor Eugene Loe called to the stand; both testified that there had been an open seat to which Rosa Parks refused to move. Professor J. E. Pierce, of Alabama State University, who worked with Parks at the local NAACP, shook his head in disgust and whispered to E. D. Nixon, who had returned from New York for the trial, "You can always find some damn white woman to lie."

The trial of Rosa Parks lasted only five minutes. Prosecutor Loe did not argue the case on the "open seat" question; instead, he simply clung to a 1945 state law that accorded Alabama bus drivers unlimited power to enforce segregation ordinances. Fred Gray did his best to challenge the validity of the segregation law, to no avail. When the gavel came down, Rosa Parks was a convicted criminal and was fined ten dollars plus another four in court costs. The swelling crowd of blacks outside city hall let out a collective moan of disgust when they heard the verdict, but they refused to just go home. Instead, a mass meeting was called for that evening at Holt Street Baptist Church to rally behind Rosa Parks.

After the crowd at city hall dispersed, Nixon, Abernathy, and the Reverend Edgar N. French, a young minister from Hilliard Chapel AME Zion Church, convened over lunch to hammer out orderly agendas for that evening's mass meeting and for the bus boycott overall. They immediately agreed that the boycott should continue, then drafted a list of concessions the bus company would have to agree to before Montgomery's blacks would end it. Among the draft's conditions were adoption of Jo Ann Robinson's "ridership compromise plan," which stated that blacks would seat themselves on public conveyances from the rear forward and whites from the front backward, with the provision that no passenger would ever be required to surrender his or her seat or to stand when there was a vacant seat anywhere on the bus; that public-transportation workers be required to show courtesy to all patrons at all times; and that African Americans would be eligible to be hired as city bus drivers. Nixon, Abernathy, and French then adopted a name for a new organization that they proposed be formed to oversee the extended boycott: The Montgomery Improvement Association (MIA).

Early that afternoon, dozens of the city's black leaders assembled at the Reverend L. Roy Bennett's Mt. Zion AME Church. Timidity ran through the group. After all, as some of the more conservative ministers pointed out, the Claudette Colvin case had blown up in E. D. Nixon's face, while the number of area lynchings had fallen dramatically and race relations for the most part seemed to have settled into a tolerable status quo. The ministers worried that if they voted for the Nixon-Abernathy-French plan, the police might hound them as rabble-rousers or even Communists, and they might lose their pastorships. Some also expressed concern that there might be a police informant in their midst and that they therefore preferred to vote on any new proposals, including creating the MIA, by secret ballot. "How do you think you can run a boycott in secret?" Nixon exploded. "Let me tell you gentlemen one thing: you ministers have lived off these washwomen for the last one hundred years and ain't never done nothing for them." His rage getting the better of him, Nixon scolded the clergymen for acting like scared "little boys" and chided, "We've worn aprons all our lives. It's time to take the aprons off. . . . If we're going to be men, now's the time to be men."

What happened next, as Taylor Branch tells it in *Parting the Waters*, would forever change American society. Slipping into the meeting late, just as Nixon was unleashing his bombast, Martin Luther King, Jr., spoke up. "Brother Nixon, I'm not a coward," he interjected, in essence sticking up for the other preachers. "I don't want anybody to call me a coward." Then, with quiet authority, he added that he agreed with Nixon that the group should vote openly and let their names be recorded in one column or the other for history's sake. With that, Coach Rufus Lewis, a burly mortician and uncompromising firebrand when it came to civil rights, took the floor and nominated King as the first president of the new MIA, pulling the plug on E. D. Nixon's ambitions. Without missing a beat, P. E. Conley, a funeral business cohort of Lewis's, seconded the motion. Many eyes darted nervously about the room, but nobody put forward the name of Abernathy or Nixon, who, with French, had conceived the MIA. At that moment, it became official: The mantle of leadership of the Montgomery bus boycott was dropped on Dr. Martin Luther King, Jr., an obscure young minister, seemingly unprepared to take center stage in such a national drama. His hopes for the leading role dashed, a hurt Nixon would later complain that for fifteen years he had been "pulling chestnuts out of the fire" for Montgomery's blacks and all he got in return was rejection in favor of a peach-fuzzed boy from out of state.

Meanwhile, as the men wrangled over pecking order and grand strategy, Rosa Parks spent the afternoon after her trial playing secretary in Fred Gray's office. The telephone rang nonstop with many callers inquiring about Rosa Parks; when she answered, she coyly pretended to be somebody else and took messages for the "bus martyr," promising to pass them along. Late that afternoon, E. D. Nixon, somewhat consoled at being treasurer of the MIA, picked her up and drove her home. She was pleased to learn from him on the way that King would be heading the new organization. Whether the bus boycott would continue remained uncertain, however; the people of black Montgomery would decide later that evening at the Holt Street Baptist Church. If the commitment was there, the protest would carry on. Otherwise, the infant MIA would have to come up with a new strategy. But for the moment, Rosa Parks felt blessed: The one-day boycott had been a grand success, and her court ordeal was over.

CHAPTER 8

"We Make the Road by Walking It"

OF ALL THE LARGE BLACK CHURCHES in mid-1950s Montgomery, Alabama, the huge, redbrick Holt Street Baptist Church was perhaps the least opulent. Located in the poorest part of town, just three blocks from the Cleveland Courts projects, its only outward ornaments were a line of yellow bricks around the windows and steeple of what otherwise looked like an inner-city union hall or industrial warehouse. The church was nonetheless chosen to host the post-trial rally for Rosa Parks, thanks to its cavernous interior, which recalled nothing so much as a Bavarian beer hall with pews. Holt Street Baptist also had the advantage of being deep in the city's poorest district—the west side—where few whites ever ventured.

As Rosa Parks made her way to the 7 P.M. gathering, she could hardly believe what she was seeing. Throngs of African Americans crowded around the church for blocks in each direction, forming a vast sea of people such as black Montgomery had never witnessed. A few police cars roamed the area with searchlights, but even they couldn't get near the entrance to Holt Street Baptist. Traffic was backed up in front of the church for blocks, and so many vehicles were parked haphazardly across the neighborhood's front lawns and back alleys that it looked like the afternoon of the annual

Alabama-Auburn football game. A loudspeaker system had been set up outside so that the well-behaved overflow crowd of four thousand could hear the proceedings. Inside, the church's pews were crammed with bodies. The standing-room-only balcony was packed far beyond the local fire code, dropped coats obscuring the oak railings, and all the women were wearing their best dresses; the men, their best suits. All told, about one thousand supporters had squeezed inside for the rally, many having arrived as early as 5 P.M.

The program was just beginning as Rosa Parks fought her way through the crush spilling out the door onto the front steps of the church. Eventually, she worked her way forward to her designated seat on the platform. "The main thing they wanted to decide at that meeting was whether to continue the boycott," Parks wrote in My Story. "Some people thought we should quit while we were ahead. And hardly anybody thought the boycott could go longer than the end of the week, which was four days. If it did, it could be very danger-ous, because everyone knew that whites wouldn't stand for it."

Prayers were recited and Scriptures read before E. D. Nixon cleared his throat and launched into the exhortation that the one-day bus boycott be extended into a "long-drawn-out affair." Then he turned the pulpit over to King, the new head of the new Montgomery Improvement Associ-ation. Earlier that evening King had been nervous about what he should say to this rapt crowd, but he needn't have worried: When the time came, rousing words flowed out of his trumpetlike baritone seemingly without effort. Much of his impromptu oration, delivered without notes or text, fo-cused on lauding Rosa Parks for her impeccable character and the extraordinary bravery of her David-like defiance of the Goliath known as Jim Crow. "Since it had to happen," King said of her arrest, "I'm happy it happened to a person like Rosa Parks, for nobody can doubt the boundless outreach of her integrity. Nobody can doubt the height of her character, nobody can doubt the depth of her Christian commitment." King went on: "But there comes a time that people get tired. We are here this evening to say to those who have mistreated us so long that we are tired—tired of being segregated and humiliated; tired of being kicked about by the brutal feet of oppression." To Parks's embarrassment and delight, every praise King heaped on her prompted jubilant applause. "We have no alternative but to protest," he continued, thrusting his hands forward for emphasis. "For many years we have shown amazing patience. We have sometimes given our white brothers the feeling that we liked the way we were being treated. But we come here tonight to be saved from the patience that makes us patient with anything less than freedom and justice."

King electrified the audience. To Fred Gray, the "pep talk" was reminiscent of the biblical Pentecost as described in Acts 2:1–2: "[T]hey were all with one accord in one place. And suddenly there came a sound from heaven as of a rushing mighty wind." King's speech was beyond spellbinding; it was prophetic. Some in the congregation realized for the first time that a revolution was at hand, that King was their Amos, that they were participating in a historic upheaval.

When he concluded to an ecstatic standing ovation, King immediately went over to hug the emotional Rosa Parks. "As I sat listening to the continued applause, I realized that this speech had evoked more response than any speech or sermon I had ever delivered, and yet it was virtually unprepared," King wrote later. "I came to see for the first time what the older preachers meant when they said, 'Open your mouth and God will speak for you.' " As the Reverend S. S. Seay, Jr., noted in his privately published memoir, *I Was There by the Grace of God*, King had "delivered his soul" to the assemblage in words like the "shots fired from Fort Sumter that were heard around the world."

As order was finally restored, the Reverend E. N. French introduced Parks from the rostrum, and the shouts broke out again, this time in chants of "Rosa, Rosa," punctuated by cries of "Thank you, sister." King himself would recall of that moment: "She was the heroine. They saw in her courageous person the symbol of their hopes and aspirations." Although some cried out for Parks to speak, it would have been wrong to break the spell of King's magnificent oration. Furthermore, King and the others on the platform noticed her reluctance and assured Parks that she had done enough and said enough already if she didn't want to speak.

The evening ended with Abernathy reading a three-page resolution asking for all blacks—and fair-minded whites—to stay off the buses until a deal with the city officials could be hammered out. The vote at Holt Street Baptist Church that night was unanimous to continue the boycott, to stand by Sister Rosa until she was vindicated by the law. Instead of lasting one day, as the Women's Political Council had originally planned, the Montgomery bus boycott would go on for thirteen months and would forever link the names of Martin Luther King, Jr., and Rosa Parks.

Even as King became an international star, leading the historic 1963 March on Washington and winning the 1964

Nobel Peace Prize, Parks always remained close to his heart. As other boycott leaders, such as Ralph Abernathy and E. D. Nixon, grew ever more jealous of King, Parks consistently defended him and his honor. In fact, she had come to believe that he was "special" in a way others never could be—she believed that God spoke through Martin Luther King, Jr. Returning the favor, in his book *Stride Toward Freedom* King penned perhaps the most lasting and poetic tribute ever offered about Parks's refusal to move to the back of the bus on the first day of December 1955. "It was an individual expression of a timeless longing for human dignity and freedom," he wrote. "She wasn't 'planted' there by the NAACP, or any other organization; she was planted there by her personal sense of dignity and self-respect. She was anchored to that seat by the accumulated indignities of days gone and the boundless aspirations of generations yet unborn. She was a victim of both the forces of history and the forces of destiny. She had been tracked down by the *Zeitgeist*—the spirit of the time."

It is hard now even to imagine how unknown King was before that night at the Holt Street Baptist Church or how unclear it was then that he would emerge as the nation's greatest and most enduring civil rights leader. At that point, his name had never appeared in a New York newspaper; he had not yet been awarded his Ph.D. by Boston University; his philosophy of nonviolence was only a vague, if developing, notion; his father, Dr. Martin Luther King, Sr., was far better known in Baptist circles than he was; many of his 375 parishioners at Dexter Avenue Baptist Church considered him overly ambitious; and most of Montgomery's fifty thousand African Americans had never even heard of him. Those who claim that they knew King was destined for greatness before he made his December 5, 1955, speech are engaging in revisionist recollection. As the *Montgomery Advertiser's* Joe Azbell, who covered the rally that evening, later said: Before the speech, King was just another run-of-the-mill black preacher; after it, he became "a flame that would go across America."

The first time Rosa Parks's name appeared in the national press was on December 6—the day after her trial and the Holt Street Baptist Church rally—in a small piece on the boycott on page 31 of the *New York Times*, where the item was dwarfed by a large ad for Cadillacs. To the readers of the *Times*, Parks became the "Negro seamstress" who kept her bus seat; but in Montgomery, her quasi canonization was already under way. As boycott participant Inez Baskin noted later, most already considered Parks "an angel walking"—a "heaven-sent" messenger. The majority of historians have ascribed the success of the Montgomery bus boycott to King's extraordinary gift for leadership; the tightly condensed layout of the city; blunders by Montgomery's white city officials; and the large number of the city's blacks who owned cars and thus didn't have to rely on public transportation. All of these were undeniably contributing factors, but so was Parks's spiritual presence. In many ways the 1955–56 Montgomery bus boycott was a crusade. And to have Parks, the epitome of a good Christian woman, as a rallying symbol made it far easier for the ministers to bolster morale. If a day laborer's feet got so tired that he thought of riding the bus, all he had to do was mutter, "Rosa Parks," and the temptation would be gone. While NAACP members in the North saw Parks as an ordinary woman who one day did an extraordinary thing, in

Montgomery she was regarded as a divine messenger. As Fred Gray would write, "She gave me the feeling that I was the Moses that God had sent to Pharaoh." It helped, of course, that at forty-two years old Parks was also a natural maternal figure to the young ministers and lawyers who led the boycott: Gray was only twenty-five, King was twenty-six, and Abernathy was twenty-nine.

As Christmas approached, the boycott continued while the MIA, operating out of a small office on Union Street, tried to negotiate a settlement with city and bus company officials to no avail. The organization's main concern was police brutality: Rogue cops were routinely arresting black car poolers and harassing African Americans waiting at taxi stands. In addition, the city's 210 black cabdrivers were regularly threatened with fines if they didn't charge every passenger the minimum forty-five-cent fare. African Americans' homes were often raided without cause, their Fourth Amendment rights notwithstanding; threats and intimidation became the city's most effective tactics against the boycott. Meanwhile, Montgomery's explosion of black pride was triggering a backlash of anxiety from the White Citizens Council and the Ku Klux Klan, adding the prospect of violence to the already volatile atmosphere. "Our weapons are protest and love," King would say. "We are going to fight until we take the heart out of Dixie."

On December 8, MIA officials, including King and Gray, met with city commissioners and bus-company officials to make it clear that blacks were not seeking an end to segregation with their boycott. Instead, King reasonably presented the MIA's demands: courtesy toward African Americans on the part of bus drivers, the hiring of black bus drivers, and segregated seating on a first-come, first-served basis. To underline the legitimacy of these demands, Gray reminded the white officials that Alabama's own Mobile, among other southern cities, had already implemented, without incident, the very same seating system the MIA was advocating. The discussions went nowhere. As archsegregationist City Commissioner Clyde Sellers summed up for the white side: "If we grant the Negroes these demands, they would go about boasting of a victory that they had won over the white people, and this we will not stand for."

Thus, the battle lines were drawn, and the opposing sides dug in for a high-stakes round of brinksmanship. Nobody knew which would be the first to crack. The biggest problem was coordinating alternate transportation for all the city's blacks. King made himself into a historian of the June 1953 Baton Rouge bus boycott, studying the logistical intricacies of that showdown like a Civil War scholar dissecting Antietam. After a long conversation with the Reverend T. J. Jemison about what could be learned from the Baton Rouge experience, King proved instrumental in creating a complex system of car pools and private taxis, augmented by the MIA's purchase of nearly a dozen station wagons. Many Montgomery blacks prosperous enough to own cars offered them to the noble cause *pro bono*. Yet as the days went by, the negotiations went nowhere; the city's race relations grew tenser by the hour as Christmas drew near and Montgomery's bus boycott surpassed Baton Rouge's in duration. "No one had any idea how long it would last," Parks recalled. "Some people said it couldn't last, but it seemed like those who said that were white people—not us. The whites did everything they could to stop it."

It was a difficult time for the embattled King, who began to question his ability to lead. It was a time of escalating hardship for Rosa Parks as well. As a member of the MIA's executive board of directors, she joined King's movement to boycott white-owned stores at the height of the Christmas shopping season and to give the money saved to the growing transportation fund instead. "We celebrated a more traditional, less commercial Christmas" that year, Parks remembered. But things got worse on January 7, 1956, when the inevitable occurred: Montgomery Fair "discharged" her not because of the boycott, the department store said, but because it was closing the tailor shop she worked in. The store gave Parks two weeks' severance pay plus the bonus money she had earned and bade her farewell. "This was a blessing in a way," she said later, "because then I didn't have to worry about how I was going to get to and from work without riding the buses."

She began working at home instead, taking in sewing jobs in between attending various MIA and St. Paul AME Church functions. A more unexpected—and financially devastating—blow followed the next week, however, when a furious Raymond Parks quit his job at Maxwell Air Force Base after his boss, William Armstrong, issued an order prohibiting any discussion of the bus boycott or of "Rosa" in the privately owned barbershop. Raymond Parks simply, and justifiably, could not work at a place where the mere mention of his own wife's name was grounds for firing. Making matters worse, the Parks's white landlord raised their rent by ten dollars a month. Depressed, bitter, worried, and unable to procure meaningful employment in the segregated South—reduced to answering death threats on the telephone while

Rosa attended boycott functions—Raymond, who had always had a fondness for gin, began drinking heavily and chain-smoking to cope with his depression. "It is fine to be a heroine," Virginia Durr wrote Myles Horton about Rosa's struggles, "but the price is high."

So the Parks family confronted the damp and bitter cold of January 1956 without full-time employment—which is not to say that Rosa wasn't working full-time. She roved all over Montgomery that winter, lending whatever help she could wherever it was needed most. Periodically she worked the ham radio as a dispatcher for the MIA Transportation Committee, directing taxi drivers and the church station-wagon crew to urgent pickups at thirty-two designated sites. There were a few long, grueling days in which Rosa Parks dispatched drivers from 5:30 in the morning until midnight, seeing to it that Montgomery's thirty thousand black boycotters found ways to and from work, school, and church. She also distributed food and clothing to make sure the poor folks who lost their jobs because of the boycott were taken care of, behaving more like a Goodwill or Salvation Army worker then an unemployed person herself. After the *New York Times* ran a story on January 8 headlined "Negroes' Boycott Cripples Bus Line," followed a few days later by a photograph of the Reverend Robert Graetz shaking hands in solidarity with a black boycotter, hundreds of gifts came pouring into the MIA's headquarters, now located on Dorsey Street, most of them addressed to Rosa Parks. Shoes were the most common offering, and Parks delighted in matching her friends' sizes and passing out the bounty. It's little wonder that shoes were what supporters from afar assumed the black boycotters needed most: All over the world Montgomery was becoming known as "the Walking City"—and to people of color everywhere, it sounded like no less than a new Jerusalem.

Parks was not the only woman fighting to keep the boycott going. Jo Ann Robinson was in her usual overdrive, managing every facet of the protest, from editing the newsletter to driving one of the car pools every day. As Graetz later put it, the "maids were the soldiers," while King boosted everyone's morale with stories of the chaos the boycott was wreaking in white households across the city. It was the women who came up with a succession of ingenious ways to keep the boycott alive, from potluck dinners to a Valentine's Day dance. Midwife Georgia Gilmore, for example, took it upon herself to form the "Club from Nowhere," which sold baked goods and sandwiches to raise funds for the MIA. As MIA financial secretary Ema Dungee recalled, it was women activists who "passed the ideas to men to a great extent."

Running the Montgomery bus boycott was not, of course, all bake sales and jokes at the expense of whites. In addition to the nightmare of coordinating all the alternative transportation, the MIA's leaders had to be on constant lookout for dirty tricks by the other side. In one ploy, on January 21, city officials claimed to have struck a deal to end the boycott with three black ministers who represented rural churches on the outskirts of town—and who did not belong to the MIA. Using that Saturday's *Montgomery Advertiser* as the vehicle for their ruse, the commissioners were convinced that their lie would be believed and that come Monday, the city's buses would again be full of black faces toward the back.

It didn't work. Noted African-American journalist and then *Minneapolis Tribune* reporter Carl T. Rowan, who in 1951 had written a devastatingly brilliant attack on Jim

Crow, *South to Freedom*, telephoned King from Minnesota to say he was perplexed by a wire-service story that had come over the *Tribune* ticker reporting that the Montgomery bus boycott was over. The wire's bogus item was news to King, who immediately began a hurry-up offensive, cruising Saturday-night juke joints with Abernathy and telling the revelers to disregard all rumors and to keep on walking. They then made sure every black minister in the MIA knew that there was no "settlement" and to instruct their Sunday congregations to keep walking come Monday.

When Montgomery's entire black community did just that the next day, an embarrassed Mayor Gayle decided that the best way to bust the boycott now was to turn up the heat on African Americans. In a desperation move, Gayle denounced the MIA as a "group of Negro radicals," claimed he was tired of "pussyfooting around," refused to negotiate anymore, and ordered his police force to "get tough" with the boycotters. This new hard line sent a shiver up the spine of the protesters: A new era of city-sponsored harassment was at hand. With the mayor refusing ever to talk again with what he dismissed as the rabble-rouser King and his MIA cronies, the gamble had suddenly turned winner-take-all. The question remained which side would fold its hand first.

That evening, the MIA held a mass meeting at Beulah Baptist Church. The assembly voted for a reaffirmation of support for the boycott, but everyone in attendance seemed on edge. Rightly so, it turned out: The next day, the city commissioners extended the Montgomery City Lines bus franchise for another ten years. And at the company's request a fare increase was approved: Adult prices were raised a nickel, to fifteen cents. It was going to be a long winter.

But on January 26, what appears to be spiritual destiny collided with what was certainly foolishness on the part of city officials: The Montgomery police arrested Martin Luther King, Jr., for driving thirty miles an hour in a twenty-five-mile-per-hour zone. The officers frisked him, tossed him in the back of their squad car, and hauled him to the station, where they took his fingerprints and mug shots and then threw the doctoral candidate from Boston University into a fetid holding cell like a common criminal. Abernathy, Parks, and other boycott leaders were indignant and immediately demanded King's release. A crowd quickly swelled around the city jail. Wisely, the police decided it was best to let King go before a race riot broke out.

The following evening, his confidence rattled by his arrest and still eroding, King had his first profound "religious experience." What triggered the epiphany was a death threat by telephone at midnight. The caller said: "Nigger, we are tired of you and your mess now. And if you aren't out of town in three days, we're going to blow your brains out and blow up your house."

Over the preceding weeks King had received several death threats, but there was something more ominous in this one. He thought about his wife, Coretta, and the real dangers to which his MIA activities were exposing her. He contemplated life without his two-month-old baby daughter, Yoki, the apple of his eye. Was it fair or right, he wondered, to risk their lives for Rosa Parks? Did it really matter that much who got to sit where on the bus? Was it proper to disobey his father, who wanted him to return to Atlanta?

With his head bowed over a cup of coffee, King prayed out loud to God to give him strength, to tell him what to do.

And at that moment, as King told the story later in *Stride Toward Freedom*, he "heard an 'inner voice' saying, 'Martin Luther, stand up for righteousness. Stand up for justice. Stand up for truth. And lo, I will be with you, even until the end of the world.' . . . I heard the voice of Jesus saying still to fight on. He promised never to leave me, never to leave me alone. No, never alone."

At around the same time, Rosa Parks had a similar "born again" moment. While praying in a pew at St. Paul AME, she suddenly felt a blessing from God sweep over her, lifting the burdens from her soul and salving her earthly cares. She came away from the church feeling lighthearted, confident that the strange combination of circumstances that had put her at the vortex of a major civil rights struggle was the work of the Lord. She emerged from St. Paul AME convinced that the time for moral courage and universal love had come for Montgomery; she could hear the chimes of freedom ringing, and all she had to do was "keep the faith." Like King's, Rosa Parks's mind was no longer troubled, her conscience just as suddenly uncluttered. "True peace of mind had swept over me," Parks recalled.

Two days later, on January 30, King had finished speaking to the regular Monday meeting of the MIA at Abernathy's First Baptist Church and was passing the collection plate for more transportation funds when he was informed that a bomb had exploded at his house on Jackson Street. Calmly stepping back to the podium, in a soft, reassuring voice, King told the congregation that he needed to go home to make sure his wife and daughter were all right. "My religious experience a few nights before had given me the strength to face it," he would explain later.

By the time he reached the parsonage, a few hundred people had gathered in silence on his front lawn amid the police lights flashing in all directions. A determined King raced through the crowd and into the house, where he couldn't stop hugging his wife and kissing his baby, neither of whom had been hurt. The explosion had, however, blown out all his front windows and left a crater in the concrete floor of the porch.

Police Commissioner Sellers and Mayor Gayle were already on the scene, trying to bring order to a crowd growing more vengeful by the minute. In a majestic display of composure, King addressed the onlookers, exhorting them to cast off despair, to abjure the evil temptations of revenge, and to "love our enemies." Then he urged everyone to go home, but not before adding that were he actually to be killed someday, others would have to seize the torch and carry on the fight for equal rights for all Americans, no matter the color of their skin. Even Sellers and Gayle were moved by the oratory of this fearless young preacher. The crowd broke into a rendition of "Amazing Grace."

The bombing of King's house marked a turning point for the MIA, and its executive board moved forward the following morning with their plan to file a federal lawsuit challenging the constitutionality of city and state bus-segregation laws. It was Clifford Durr, in fact, who had convinced the MIA that appealing Rosa Parks's December 5 conviction was not an appropriate vehicle for challenging the segregation provisions. Her appeal would have to go through the Alabama state courts before it could reach the U.S. Supreme Court, making delaying tactics and other chicanery probable. Even more problematic were the circumstances of Rosa

Parks's arrest: Because she had refused to move when there was no other seat available on the bus, Durr could foresee her conviction being overturned without the issue of segregation even being discussed, much less resolved. So, following Durr's advice, attorneys Fred Gray and Charles Langford filed a petition with the U.S. District Court on behalf of four female plaintiffs—including Claudette Colvin and Mary Louise Smith—who had been mistreated on the buses. They were prepared to argue their case before Chief Justice Earl Warren himself, if necessary, on the grounds set out in the *Brown* ruling: that "separate but equal" was unconstitutional. In the meantime, Parks's appeal was dismissed on a technicality and her conviction thus upheld. She was guilty in the eyes of Alabama.

News of the MIA's *Browder v. Gayle* case enraged white city officials, who hadn't been able to regain their upper hand since Parks's arrest two months earlier. The black community's spirit had been soaring the whole while as scores of international journalists came pouring into Montgomery on assignment. Stories about the "tired seamstress" who kept her seat appeared in newspapers from Calcutta to Buenos Aires to Manila. Parks received flowers from Bolivia, shoes from Sweden, prayer beads from India. The bus boycott itself continued to be economically effective; not only was it bankrupting Montgomery City Lines with losses of over a thousand dollars a day, but white downtown business owners had begun to complain that the intransigence of city officials was costing them substantial revenues in lost sales to black clients and shoppers. And in only six weeks or so, warm weather would return to Alabama, the migratory birds would head north, and walking to work and doing errands would become less arduous for the boycotters.

The ongoing success of the blacks' protest bred frustration among Montgomery's whites, which began to fester into violence. With few guns to protect themselves, only an untried philosophy of nonviolence, African Americans grew increasingly worried that the situation would soon turn ugly and even that King might be assassinated. Floodlights were installed in front of his parsonage, and the men of Dexter Avenue Baptist Church organized a sundown-to-sunup guard for his home. As these new security measures were being implemented, only one day after the explosion at King's residence, a bomb was tossed at E. D. Nixon's house, shattering windows throughout the block. "Mr. Nixon was away at the time," Parks recalled. "I rushed over to his house and helped clean up the mess, sweeping out the porch and making sure that all of his papers were in order."

Clearly, white Montgomery's rage was not going to subside, and many of the MIA's black ministers feared they would soon find themselves either lynched or locked away in an Alabama penitentiary. Tensions rose higher on February 6, when white students at the University of Alabama in nearby Tuscaloosa rioted to protest the court-ordered admission of the school's first black student, Autherine Lucy. Fearful of mob violence breaking out, the college's board of trustees decided to bar Lucy from attending classes "for her own safety" and later expelled her. The open defiance of *Brown* notched a major victory for states' rights regarding segregation and rolled a tidal wave of its effect over Montgomery. Just four days later, more than ten thousand whites from across Alabama and Mississippi gathered at the Montgomery Coliseum for the biggest pro-segregation rally in the United States since the Civil War. The speakers at this White Citizens Convocation—an extravaganza anchored by hundreds of Confederate flags and regular singing rounds of "Dixie"—boasted that they would "give the niggers a whipping" and teach Rosa Parks a "harsh lesson." Keynote speaker Senator James Eastland of Mississippi—who a few years earlier had smeared the Durrs as Communists—declared that the only "prescription for victory" was for southern whites to "organize and be militant."

Three days after the white supremacist rally, Circuit Judge Eugene Carter ordered a Montgomery County grand jury to determine whether King, Parks, Abernathy, and other black community leaders were violating a 1921 statute outlawing boycotts "without just cause or legal excuse." Prosecutors summoned more than two hundred African-American witnesses to testify about who was behind the boycott. The word "indictment" swept into hushed conversations across the west side of Montgomery as poor blacks worried they would soon find themselves breaking rocks on prison chain gangs simply because they had been walking to work. The police actually did arrest Fred Gray on February 18, fingerprinting him on the ridiculous charge of "barratry," the criminal offense of habitually initiating lawsuits, insisting that one of the plaintiffs in the *Browder* case against the city, Jeanetta Reese, had never authorized him to use her name. Under police intimidation and fearful for her life, Reese had indeed withdrawn as a plaintiff; but the charge against Gray was dismissed on March 2. As Joe Azbell noted in the *Adver-*

tiser, Montgomery was teetering on the brink of a "full-scale racial war."

The gavel of injustice fell on Rosa Parks again on the afternoon of February 21, when the Montgomery County grand jury indicted her and eighty-eight others—including King and twenty other ministers—for violating the 1921 Alabama state statute barring boycotts. It was, according to Taylor Branch, "the largest wholesale indictment in the history of the country." Fortunately, Parks's resolve had been bolstered the day before by a warm telegram from Myles Horton stating, "How proud we were of your courageous role in the boycott," and inviting her to Highlander two weeks hence. "I was very sorry to learn from a letter from Virginia Durr today that you had lost your job," Horton added. "Doing what's right is not always the easy thing to do. But all of us together should be able to manage somehow. Perhaps we can help."

Horton's telegram made Rosa Parks pause to remember that only six months had passed since she was sipping lemonade and chatting with Septima Clark in rural Tennessee while their fellows at Highlander sang folk tunes about "overcoming" white supremacy. Now she was unemployed, her marriage was strained, and her quiet life was gone, all because she had become an accidental martyr. She reflected on how startling it was to receive kind letters from Ghana and supportive telegrams from Paris, and she wondered who would ever have dreamed that the *New York Herald Tribune* and *Time* would be telephoning apartment 634 at the Cleveland Courts projects, asking her for interviews and commentary on civil rights. She instinctively saw fame as a pitfall to avoid, worried that others were jealous of her unwanted celebrity. She mastered the art of self-deprecation as a survival mechanism.

But Rosa Parks never felt alone. Who, she reminded herself, could ask for a defender as brave as E. D. Nixon, a lawyer as dedicated as Fred Gray, a white friend as loyal as Virginia Durr, a minister as passionate as Martin Luther King, Jr., a neighbor as tenderhearted as Robert Graetz, a mentor as inspiring as Septima Clark, a radical backer as tireless as Myles Horton, a friend as funny as Johnnie Mae Carr, or a church congregation as sympathetic as St. Paul AME's? Feeling all their strength behind her, Parks was calm when she learned of her indictment the day after she got Horton's letter. She would not wait for the police to arrive and make her feel like a criminal. Following E. D. Nixon's lead, she would march into the courthouse of her own accord, ask to see the sheriff, and declare to him, "Are you looking for me? Well, I am here."

CHAPTER 9

Steadfast and Unmovable

PERHAPS THE BEST-KNOWN PHOTOGRAPH of Rosa Parks is one taken on February 22, 1956, that appeared on the front page of the *New York Times* the next day. The Associated Press photo showed a nonplussed Parks, meticulously dressed in a smart business suit, her hair pulled into a bun, being fingerprinted by a young Montgomery police officer. Over the coming years this image would be misidentified in hundreds of American history books as showing Parks during her first arrest, on December 1, 1955. Nevertheless, the 1956 photo in the *New York Times* brought Rosa Parks international recognition as a freedom fighter. Her picture rippled through civil rights movements worldwide: that spring, in South Africa, thousands boycotted the segregated buses in Cape Town in symbolic solidarity with Parks. "Before King there was Rosa Parks," then apartheid leader and later South African president Nelson Mandela later explained. "She is who inspired us, who taught us to sit down for our rights, to be fearless when facing our oppressors." And future UN secretary general Kofi Annan closely monitored the bus boycott as a schoolboy in Ghana, embracing Parks as one of his first heroes. "The fact that a woman triggered such a movement was doubly liberating," Annan recalled. "She was courageous, and in Africa we all cheered for her."

The MIA paid Parks's bail in February 1956, and the avatar of the American civil rights movement returned to the Cleveland Courts projects joking that she was now a two-time criminal. For her upcoming trial she chose as witnesses Raymond and a neighbor woman, whose own husband, in army uniform and just returned from fighting in Korea, had been shot to death in August 1950 by a white policeman. In the meantime, speaking invitations came pouring in for the "Mother of the Boycott" from all over, but particularly from AME churches and NAACP branches claiming Parks as one of their own. To keep up with her new role as MIA spokesperson, Parks struggled through Swedish economist Gunnar Myrdal's 1944 classic *American Dilemma*, urging the eradication of racial discrimination. And, as always, she read a number of newspapers and magazines daily— including the *New York Herald Tribune*, *Saturday Evening Post*, and *Pittsburgh Courier*—to stay abreast of the civil rights battles being waged in other Jim Crow cities, such as Richmond and Dallas, both of which would end segregated bus seating that April. She fastidiously clipped articles not only on civil rights and the NAACP but on other interests, from Paul Robeson to gospel music to African decolonization. She saved, for example, the January 25, 1955, issue of *Look* magazine for Jackie Robinson's article about integrating baseball, "Now I Know Why They Boo Me," on which she vigorously underlined and starred his line "I never waited to shake Dixie's hand."

It's hard to imagine that anybody in Montgomery during the boycott—the Durrs included—was monitoring what Myrdal called the "Negro problem" in the popular press as scrupulously as Rosa Parks. This gives the lie to the all-too-frequent portrayal of her as an "uninformed seamstress" rather than a true intellectual leader like Martin Luther King, Jr., or Fred Gray. Although Parks lacked a university degree, it is important to remember what an exceptionally well informed citizen she was, how broad a network of worldly friends she maintained, and how many college-educated NAACP leaders considered her an equal and an irreplaceable comrade. She was an authentic grassroots activist smart enough to adopt the realistic tactics of Elizabeth Cady Stanton, not—as poet Nikki Giovanni would describe in "The Dance Committee"—some "token Negro" who sat in the "colored section with Fanon in her hand" as proof of her militancy.

The mass indictments of black leaders in February 1956 brought more than media attention to Montgomery: Pacifist activists Bayard Rustin and Glenn E. Smiley came to town from New York espousing Gandhian nonviolence and the belief that one individual could neutralize the hatred of millions by achieving "perfect love." Parks never got to know the flamboyant Rustin, who was forced to leave Alabama after the editor of a black Birmingham newspaper threatened to expose his homosexual activities and leftist associations; but she forged a solid friendship with Smiley, a white Texan official of the Fellowship of Reconciliation (FOR), who would spend the next year tutoring Martin Luther King, Jr., in strategies for peaceful civil disobedience. With spring coming, Parks and Smiley worked together to find cheap bicycles for the MIA and took a scouting trip to Atlanta to acquire a truckful of used ones. When nineteen U.S. senators and eighty-two House members issued a "Southern Manifesto" on March 12 denouncing the Supreme Court's *Brown* decision and other desegregation rulings, the Parks-Smiley team coauthored an unsigned MIA statement denouncing the manifesto as an "inflammatory gesture."

The trials of Parks and other MIA coconspirators were set to begin on March 19 at the Montgomery Circuit Court. As it turned out, however, King was the only one actually tried. After four days of testimony from sixty witnesses, including the Parks's neighbor whose husband had been shot by a policeman, Judge Eugene Carter found the defendant guilty and sentenced him either to pay a five-hundred-dollar fine or serve 386 days in prison at hard labor. Despite the verdict, when he emerged from the courthouse, King was cheered by Parks and hundreds of other African Americans, as though he really were what *Jet* magazine had just called him: "Alabama's Modern Moses." King would lose his state appeal and be forced to pay the five-hundred-dollar fine in November 1957, but his unfair conviction only enhanced his status as a civil rights martyr. "From that day onward Parks became a secondary figure," Rufus Lewis noted later.

As the boycott continued in the wake of King's trial, MIA members pinned their hopes on the Montgomery district court's upcoming hearing on the *Browder v. Gayle* lawsuit challenging Alabama's bus segregation laws. On May 11, Fred Gray's three remaining female plaintiffs began testifying before a three-judge panel. When sixteen-year-old Claudette Colvin was cross-examined about who had instigated the bus boycott and who its leaders were now, in a quiet voice she answered: "Our leaders is just we ourselves." The MIA believed that appellate judge Richard Rives was on their side, while district judge Seyborn H. Lynne probably was not. This left the boycott's future on district judge Frank M. Johnson,

Jr., a World War II veteran who had been seriously wounded five days into the D-day invasion at Normandy and later became the youngest federal judge in the country when President Eisenhower appointed him to the bench at age thirty-seven in 1955.

Curious to know more about the man who would determine their next course, the MIA looked into Johnson's background and turned up some encouraging facts: The judge was a native of Alabama's progressive Winston County—which had considered seceding from the state over slavery during the Civil War and ended up sending more men to serve in the Union Army than on the Confederate side—and was a self-styled "conservative hillbilly" known for his fair-mindedness. Johnson had graduated first in his class from the University of Alabama's law school in 1943 and had established a reputation in Tuscaloosa as an unapologetic judicial activist who admired the liberal Supreme Court justices Louis Brandeis and Felix Frankfurter. Parks remembered that Earl Warren had been a conservative Republican governor of California before he grew into the chief justice of the United States who presided over *Brown v. Board of Education of Topeka;* maybe Johnson, another member of the party of Abraham Lincoln, would prove equally progressive. She also heard promising stories about the judge through the Alabama preacher's grapevine, primarily from Birmingham's Fred Shuttleworth and Joseph Lowery of Mobile. "My fingers were crossed and I prayed," Parks recalled. "And as it turned out, he proved to be a genuine champion of justice."

On June 5, 1956, six weeks after the hearing, the judges ruled two to one in favor of the plaintiffs in *Browder v. Gayle,* with Johnson's the deciding vote, as expected. To the delight of Parks and every other black Alabaman, the majority opinion written by Johnson held that the *Brown* decision's rejection of the "separate but equal" doctrine reached beyond public school segregation to other forms of Jim Crow. The court thus pronounced the Montgomery and Alabama bus segregation statutes unconstitutional, as violations of the Fourteenth Amendment's due process and equal protection clause. It was a stunning landmark decision, and wild jubilation erupted across black Montgomery as if Joe Louis had just knocked out an entire battalion of Max Schmelings. Although he was as ecstatic as anyone, Fred Gray—who had gotten married just two days earlier—cautioned Rosa and Raymond Parks and all the rest to keep their celebrating in check: Montgomery's city commissioners were, as expected, appealing the case to the U.S. Supreme Court. The boycott would have to continue until the fall at least.

Through the rest of the spring of 1956, Parks, King, Abernathy, Nixon, and other leaders traveled the country raising funds for the MIA as the organization's "speakers's bureau." That May, Rosa Parks boarded an airplane for the first time in her life to fly to New York—on the Highlander School's nickel—to speak at a rally at Madison Square Garden. Parks was squired around Manhattan for two weeks, staying first with a Quaker couple, Charlotte and Steward Meacham, for a few days and then by herself in a small room at the Henry Street Settlement on the city's Lower East Side. She toured Harlem with Ella Baker, dined in Chinatown, and listened to jazz in Greenwich Village. Everywhere she went, African Americans greeted her as a heroine, asking her for her autograph and to pose for pictures. She was praised at black churches and toasted at Lenox Avenue bars. While in New

York, Parks got to meet three of her own idols: A. Philip Randolph, NAACP head Roy Wilkins, and Eleanor Roosevelt, who praised the civil rights activist in her syndicated newspaper column on May 14. "A few days ago I met Rosa Parks, who started the nonviolent protest in Montgomery, Alabama, against segregation on buses," the former first lady wrote in her "My Day" column. "She is a very quiet, gentle person and it is difficult to imagine how she ever could take such a positive and independent stand." It was heady stuff for a seamstress who had grown up on the wrong side of Jim Crow in rural Alabama. But instead of enjoying the adulation, Parks was beginning to develop the stomach ulcers that would continue to plague her in coming years.

She enjoyed a respite on the speaking tour's stop in Detroit, where she stayed with her brother, Sylvester, who still worked at a Chrysler Motor Company plant. E. D. Nixon had raised thirty-five thousand dollars in the city when he had addressed a convention of local United Automobile Workers union presidents in March; now it was Parks's task to raise funds at the Motor City's various AME and Baptist churches, and she came though, netting six thousand dollars for the cause over three days. But by the time Parks reached San Francisco in early June for the forty-seventh annual NAACP national convention, her nerves were frayed. Suffering from chronic insomnia, jet lag, burning stomach ulcers, and homesickness, she was not in good shape, as would soon become clear.

Throughout the trip Parks had acquitted herself graciously and had almost become used to speaking about Montgomery's new civil war on various radio shows and to newspaper reporters. Unfortunately, given the state of her health, in the supposed liberal bastion of San Francisco, Parks was confronted by a racist reporter who accused her of being a publicity-seeking phony. "I was trying my best to answer this man's questions, but evidently I wasn't saying what he wanted me to say or something," Parks recalled. "He was a white reporter, and I remember one of the first things he said was 'Don't stare at me.' I thought I was looking straight at him. Well, that got me nervous. Then he announced arrogantly that he was going 'to take me apart and see what made me tick.' He was trying to intimidate me, and he succeeded."

The reporter launched a barrage of harsh, sexist questions at Parks, including one asking whether she had ever worked as a prostitute. The teacup in Parks's hand began rattling against its saucer. Unable to stand her interrogator's "obnoxious" line of questioning, Parks flew into "hysterics," in her own word, screaming and crying. The reporter smirked at her, offered her a mocking "bye-bye," and walked away. Parks sat bawling on a sofa in the hotel lobby where the interview took place for half an hour until Roy Wilkins saw her, sat down at her side, put his arm around her, and said reassuringly "It's all right, Rosa," over and over again.

But that encounter in San Francisco was the only reported bad experience of Parks's travels. At the other extreme was her reception at various AME churches, where she found herself lionized as a "Black Madonna." This grew out of the commonplace practice in AME churches of envisioning God and Jesus as dark-skinned, a concept Parks heartily approved. It had been back in 1898 that AME clergymen Henry McNeal Turner declared, in his famous address "God Is a Negro," that it was "better to hang our gospel trumpet upon the willow and cease to preach" than to continue to propagate the notion that Christ was white. During World War I this notion was underlined by the Reverend Alexander McGuire, a black Episcopalian priest who worked closely with radical separatist Marcus Garvey, when he begged African Americans to "forget the white gods, erase the white gods from your mind." Following this holy summons, many AME churches pulled down their blue-eyed, blond Jesuses like so many Lenin statues in Russia after the cold war and replaced them with black versions. Theologian C. Eric Lincoln pointed out in his 1974 book *The Black Church Since Frazier* that beginning in the 1920s, the image of the "Black Madonna and Child" became popular in many race-conscious African-American homes and churches and was widely reproduced on wall calendars, book covers, and holiday greeting cards. In the spring of 1956 a succession of AME churches along MIA's itinerary suddenly met a Black Madonna in the flesh.

Upon returning to Montgomery in late June, Parks's heart sank when she saw how sick her mother was, how heavily her husband was drinking, and how many bills had been left unpaid. Having not been offered speaking fees, only travel expenses, Parks found herself in debt for the first time in her life and was ashamed when she eventually had to accept six hundred dollars from Virginia and Clifford Durr. Meanwhile, hate mail arrived every day at 634 Cleveland Court, and Bertha Butler often talked on the telephone for hours with Leona McCauley so that Raymond Parks wouldn't have to answer any more "Die, nigger" calls at night. The White Citizens Council was still trying to derail the bus boycott, this time by persuading automobile-insurance companies to refuse to cover the MIA's station wagons, or "rolling churches," as they were mocked. Four times in as many months the association had its policies canceled, which could have been disastrous to the boycott had the resourceful King not managed to arrange insurance with a black-owned company in Atlanta that counted Lloyd's of London among its underwriters.

With her financial troubles at bay for the moment, Parks returned to the Highlander Folk School that August to celebrate the first anniversary of her first visit with a weeklong workshop. She rode to the Tennessee mountain retreat in Reverend Robert Graetz's light blue 1955 Chevy along with Graetz's wife, Jeannie, and their three kids, making the two-hundred-mile journey what Parks called a "family affair." Once in Monteagle, Parks thrilled at reconnecting with Myles Horton, Septima Clark, and Ella Baker and thoroughly enjoyed the week. But the reunion ended with disturbing news. Early on the morning of Saturday, August 25, the last day of the workshop, a Highlander staffer came knocking on Graetz's cabin door to deliver a message from Tom Pastor, a black reporter for the *New York Post:* Two sticks of dynamite had been tossed into Graetz's front yard in Montgomery and exploded, knocking out windows and inflicting other minor damage. Everyone at Highlander gathered for a prayer session and sang "We Shall Not Be Moved," holding hands. It was a poignant good-bye.

Graetz was loathed perhaps more than any other boycott leader by Montgomery's whites, who saw him as a left-wing "nigger lover." Earlier that year, sugar had been poured into his car's gasoline tank and two of its tires slashed. Two automobile-insurance companies had canceled his policies, and telephone death threats had become an everyday occurrence. Now, to Graetz's even greater chagrin, the Montgomery police used the bombing of his house to confiscate all his personal records and correspondence, the mayor even telling reporters that the minister had probably hurled the dynamite himself for a publicity stunt. An enraged Martin Luther King, Jr., who had grown quite fond of Graetz, immediately fired off a letter to President Eisenhower protesting that Montgomery's bus boycotters were now "without protection of law." On September 4, Graetz himself wrote a letter to U.S. attorney general Herbert Brownell, Jr., requesting that the Justice Department investigate Mayor W. A. Gayle's police force for possible gross negligence and perhaps even criminal charges related to the bombing. Nothing ever came of it.

Throughout that fall Rosa Parks, like all the other boycotters, waited patiently for the Supreme Court's decision in the *Browder* case, meanwhile continuing to keep the minutes at some MIA meetings and heading the organization's Publicity Committee. At last, and just a week after President Dwight D. Eisenhower was reelected in a landslide over Democrat Adlai Stevenson—with the help of a surprising 60 percent of African Americans—justice came to Montgomery. On November 13, 1956, the U.S. Supreme Court upheld without dissent the federal district court's *Browder v. Gayle* decision striking down Alabama's segregation laws. "The universe is on the side of justice," a triumphant King declared as black Montgomery broke into a euphoria of singing church choirs and honking car horns. Robed Ku Klux Klan members drove through black neighborhoods hoping to intimidate the residents, but their posses met only ridicule from teenagers and jeering old women. Scared, the Klansmen fled the black neighborhoods, more bitter than ever. But once again MIA leaders had to rein back the celebration: in a last-ditch effort, the city of Montgomery was petitioning the high court for reconsideration, and it would be another month before the appeal was dismissed and bus desegregation became the law.

In the interim, on November 14, Parks left Montgomery on a new, weeklong NAACP fund-raising foray to Chicago and New York. While she was away, Virginia Durr wrote to Myles Horton exhorting him to put Parks on a thirty-five-dollar-a-month retainer from Highlander to operate a Voters' Service Bureau in Montgomery, out of Fred Gray's law office behind the Sears, Roebuck store. "Rosa has left on tour for the NAACP and will end it up on the 20th," Durr began her appeal, adding, "I wish you could be in New York when she gets there, as she needs direction; she is timid and shy and yet has the courage of a lion." Horton replied that he would be unable to assist Parks in New York or put her on a monthly stipend for her work in Montgomery, but he extended her an immediate invitation back to the Highlander Folk School in early December to meet with six black students from Clinton, Tennessee, who were trying to integrate their all-white schools with no help from the local police. Parks accepted without hesitation.

Thus, in early December, while King was holding another spectacular mass meeting at Holt Street Baptist Church to thank the fifteen hundred assembled for following him, E. D. Nixon was driving Rosa Parks and her mother to Monteagle, Tennessee. "It was a rather unpleasant ride," Parks recalled. "Mr. Nixon was completely fed up with King and down on the MIA." Once they reached their destination, however, the mood brightened. Everybody at the school, including Septima Clark, turned out to greet Parks like a conquering heroine, teasing her about her world fame and later reading Psalms 27 and 33 in her honor. Later in the week, Horton offered Parks a full-time job at Highlander, asking her to move to Monteagle to teach the principles of nonviolent resistance to the teenagers from Clinton and every other town ready to integrate its schools and buses. But "Mama said no," Parks recounted. "She didn't want to be 'nowhere I don't see nothing but white folks,' so that ended that. Anyway, I was in no position to take off from Montgomery and stay somewhere else at that time."

Parks returned to a Montgomery lit up for Christmas, the MIA's free car pools still operating like clockwork. St. Paul AME had a holiday creche set up near its altar, and Parks carefully washed and dusted its ceramic figurines before each Sunday service, taking particular care that Christmas season always to lay the baby Jesus just right in his straw manger. Years later, she remembered that when she sang "Silent Night" that winter, she felt the power of God in the refrain "all is calm, all is bright." It truly had been a year of miracles. Now, with Christmas spirit all around, everybody was talking about moving away from protest and toward reconciliation. Coretta Scott King sang spirituals at an MIA benefit concert alongside Duke Ellington and Harry Belafonte at Carnegie Hall; Fred Gray was touted in black newspapers as the next Thurgood Marshall; and the Durrs' social redemption began as the McCarthy era waned. Rosa Parks considered herself blessed. And she was proved right on December 17, when the Supreme Court rejected the Montgomery City Commission's final appeal of the *Browder* decision: As of December

20, the capital's buses would be integrated by law, and the thirteen-month boycott would be over.

The limelight was already passing from Rosa Parks to Martin Luther King, Jr., upon whom the nation's television crews and print reporters descended like a flock of ravenous crows. The *New York Times* ran long front-page stories head-lined "High Court Rules Bus Segregation Unconstitutional" and "Bus Boycott's End Voted by Negroes," filled with quotes from King, in which Rosa Parks's name was not even mentioned. Hardly a glory seeker, Parks genuinely didn't mind, and she stayed home on December 21, when the buses were integrated, to take care of her ailing mother.

Not that there was anything substantive to attend to. Staged photo opportunities for the press took up most of the day, beginning at 5:45 A.M. with a fedora-topped King sitting next to Glenn Smiley in a front seat of a Montgomery city bus, presenting the perfect black-white tableau the press wanted. Although other boycott leaders, including Abernathy, were likewise photographed sitting in front of buses, Rosa Parks was never invited to join them. "Some of the books say I was with them," she said, "but I was not." At around 9:00 A.M., however, a reporter from *Look* magazine, with two photographers in tow, knocked on the Parks's apartment door and asked the woman who had sparked the boycott to come ride a bus so they could document the historic event. Despite some misgivings, Parks finally agreed and let the *Look* crew drive her to have her picture taken riding in and getting on and off buses. "I was apprehensive," Parks remembered. "But I'm glad I let them take it."

A moment of awkwardness ensued, however, when Parks boarded a Cleveland Avenue bus and saw James Blake behind the wheel. "We ignored each other," Parks recalled. "Clearly he was not interested in being photographed with me, or any other black person for that matter." Seemingly oblivious of the apparent irony, the *Look* reporter positioned Parks in a front-row seat—posing himself as a fellow passenger seated a row behind—and asked her to gaze out the window just as she had on December 1, 1955. The contrived photograph worked; over the years it has been included in history books more often than the equally ersatz shot of King and Smiley. "Children from around the world send me that picture to sign," Parks laughed years later. "It's become my symbol shot, my historical honor badge."

The process of integrating Montgomery's buses did not go well at first. After two smooth days, on December 23, a drive-by sniper fired a shotgun blast through King's front door. The next morning, the minister told his congregation at Dexter Avenue Baptist, "I would like to tell whoever did it that it won't do any good to kill me. We have just started our work." The gunfire continued regardless, buses becoming the prime targets. On Christmas Eve, five white men assaulted a fifteen-year-old African-American girl at a Montgomery bus stop. Four days later, a pregnant black woman was shot in both legs while boarding a bus, prompting the city commission to suspend all bus service after 5 P.M. Nevertheless, the violence continued into the New Year: On January 10, 1957, Ralph Abernathy's parsonage and sanctuary were both bombed, as were three other black churches in Montgomery. And once again a bomb exploded at the Reverend Graetz's house, this time causing serious damage.

But things had changed, if not enough. Seven Klansmen were arrested for the bombings, integrated buses began running without incident, and white Montgomery pined for a return to normalcy, if never again of the discriminatory sort the city was used to. That winter, an oppressive torpor shrouded downtown Montgomery, a city exhausted by the momentous events its own prejudices had spawned. In the evenings, the only sound in the city's streets was the flapping of the Confederate flag over the state capitol, forlorn in its lost cause.

Across the street from where Rosa Parks was arrested still stood the Winter Building, where the telegraph was sent granting General P. G. T. Beauregard the discretion to fire on Fort Sumter; nearby were the spots where William L. Yancey delivered his speech presenting Jefferson Davis as president-elect of the Confederacy and the portico of the capitol of Alabama, where Davis gave his inaugural address. Suddenly, however, these Confederate shrines had turned into historical embarrassments. New generations of Americans would visit Montgomery not to study Dixie lore but to see the Dexter Avenue Baptist pulpit from which Martin Luther King, Jr., had preached, the Holt Street Church where the bus boycott was organized, and the street corner on which Rosa Parks was arrested. A way of life had ended in Montgomery, and a new one had begun.

The city's mood in the wake of the bus boycott was clearly in King's hands. At a meeting in Atlanta in January 1957, a group of black Baptist preachers selected him as president of a nascent organization that would become the Southern Christian Leadership Conference (SCLC), a new, Christian-inspired civil rights consortium. Nonviolence would be the SCLC's modus operandi, not just because it was right but because it worked. As King wrote in his book *Strive*

Toward Freedom, "The story of Montgomery is the story of 50,000 Negroes who were willing to substitute tired feet for tired souls and walk the streets of Montgomery until the walls of segregation were finally battered by the forces of justice." He knew it was time to go national.

CHAPTER 10

Detroit Days

LATE ONE RAINY JULY NIGHT in 1957, Thomas Williamson—born in Alabama in 1913, just like his first cousin, Rosa
Parks—answered the phone at his house on the northeast
side of Detroit and instantly grew grim. It was "Rosie," as he
called her, struggling through tears to tell him the vicious
wording of the latest death threat against her. "Rosie, get the
hell out of Montgomery," Williamson snapped back, more in
anger than sympathy. "Raymond's right; Whitey is going to
kill you. You've got to come to Detroit, where you'll be safe."
Parks had heard the same warning nonstop over the preceding year but had paid the concerns of her friends and family
little mind. This most recent hate message, however, had a
more ominous credibility to it; in fact, it had driven Raymond Parks into a near-suicidal despair that scared his wife
more than the threat itself. "We're ready to move," Rosa
Parks finally admitted to her cousin, whom she thought of
more as a brother. "We're ready for Detroit." The next morning, Williamson went to his local bank branch, wired his
cousin three hundred dollars, and thereby brought Rosa
Parks's days in Montgomery to an end.

That August proved a sad time for Parks as she resigned
herself to the move, sold off her family's furniture, and
packed up their belongings, telling the landlord they would

be vacating 634 Cleveland Courts within two weeks. Decades later she would remember finding solace during those last days in Alabama in a passage from Matthew 20:6 that echoed her own circumstances: "So the last be first, and the first last."

The incessant death threats were the Parkses' primary reason for leaving Montgomery; the second was that the city's white business community had rendered the couple unemployable by labeling them "troublemakers." But it was the bitter resentment of their supposed friends that wounded Rosa Parks most. Before December 1955, she had been a "Girl Friday" among her African-American peers—a hardworking laborer with a civil rights bent devoted to caring for her ailing mother and husband. Then, almost literally overnight, she had become the most celebrated—and notorious—woman in Alabama history, her picture splashed across newspapers nationwide. Suddenly, Parks found herself lauded as a near saint virtually everywhere she went in black communities, and before long some of her colleagues in Montgomery's civil-rights movement began to grow jealous of the attention. She may have been first in the eyes of African Americans everywhere else, but Parks was rapidly dropping toward last in the affections of her own colleagues.

Much of the resentment sprang from male chauvinism. Even when couched in humor, to a woman as humble and demure as Parks it hurt to be teased by Baptist ministers she respected, exclaiming, "Well! If it isn't the superstar!" by way of greeting her at church functions. Even E. D. Nixon turned a cold shoulder toward her, telling Arkansas NAACP activist Daisy Bates that Parks was a "lovely, stupid woman" the media had built up into an icon. That June he finally exploded when the national NAACP office called to ask his help in getting Parks to make a speech about the Montgomery bus boycott in Washington, D.C. Nixon volunteered his own services instead and was told the national NAACP wasn't interested; they wanted Sister Rosa, and he begrudged her for it.

Similarly, the Reverend Ralph Abernathy refused to take Parks seriously as a civil rights leader, dismissing her as a mere "tool" of the MIA. He even took to gratuitously badmouthing Raymond Parks, mocking him as a frightened lush. Still flush with the success of the bus boycott, Abernathy wanted to follow up right away with a new boycott, this time of the Montgomery airport, and he bristled when Rosa Parks dared to tell him she thought it was a bad idea.

And it wasn't just the men of her acquaintance who envied her to the point of meanness: The women who had been the plaintiffs in *Browder v. Gayle*—particularly Aurelia Browder and Claudette Colvin—felt *they* deserved the public adulation, the NAACP-sponsored trips to New York, the invitations to speak, and the praise from Dr. King at least as much as she did. "We were angry that everybody was saying 'Rosa this' and 'Rosa that,'" Colvin admitted much later. "I felt ostracized by the black community."

But the pettiness turned to shame when the word hit Montgomery's black community that Rosa Parks was moving North. A repentant Ralph Abernathy visited her at Cleveland Courts, apologized for some of his recent bad behavior, and pleaded with her to stay. It was a welcome, if futile, gesture. Even more welcome, and surprising, the MIA passed a hat and raised eight hundred dollars as a going-away present. And when Rosa and Raymond Parks were honored with a farewell service at St. Paul's AME and everybody joined hands to sing a tearful "O Freedom Over Me," no one doubted that an important chapter in Montgomery's history had come to an end. "I never realized how much I would miss Rosa," Nixon later confessed. "Her leaving was a low, low moment for us all."

Thus, it was in a bittersweet mood that the Parks family moved to "Dynamic Detroit," as Rosa's brother, Sylvester, liked to call it. Detroit had been good to Sylvester McCauley since he moved to the Motor City in 1946: He had joined the United Auto Workers union and gotten a good assembly-line job at the Chrysler Corporation's Old Lynch Road Plant. He and his wife, Daisy, owned a house near River Rouge in southwest Detroit large enough to accommodate their thirteen children. In order to feed his brood, however, Sylvester planted broccoli, corn, cabbage, carrots, and okra, and even tried nursing potatoes through southeast Michigan's subzero freezes and six-foot snowstorms. "We needed a garden to keep food on the table," his oldest son, Sylvester junior, recalled. "He was good at growing. He clearly would have been a farmer if he had stayed in the South." For extra cash McCauley took freelance carpentry jobs or helped his cousin Thomas out at Williamson's cement company. "Carpentry work ran in our family," Sylvester junior related. "But the Michigan Brotherhood of Carpenters and Joiners wouldn't let father become a member because he was black." Yet not once had Rosa's brother ever thought about setting foot in— let alone moving back to—Alabama.

For their first month in Detroit, Rosa and Raymond Parks and Leona McCauley shared a bedroom upstairs at Thomas Williamson's house on Fleming Street. Then McCauley found the trio a small apartment on the west side's Euclid Avenue and built bookcases and a TV stand to make it comfortable for them, while Cousin Thomas came through with a dining-room set. It proved a nice time for Rosa Parks: she baby-sat her little nieces and nephews, established connections with the local chapters of the NAACP and Urban League, and sewed clothes to repay relatives for the generosity of their welcome. Still, as ever, money was scarce. Whenever Parks made a cup of tea, she saved the bag to use again, ate only small portions at every meal, and always brought a doggy bag home on the rare occasions the family dined out. She even kept empty cardboard paper-towel rolls to store her scarves so they wouldn't wrinkle. In coming years her nieces and nephews would jokingly dub Aunt Rosie "the Recycling Queen" and "Mrs. Thrifty."

The move to Detroit hardly checked Parks's social activism. After a month of settling into the Euclid Avenue apartment, she once again took to the road on a lecture tour. At one NAACP function in Boston in October 1957 she met Alonzo G. Moron, president of Virginia's Hampton Institute—the renowned black college on the Chesapeake Bay at which Booker T. Washington had been educated—and he quickly offered her the position of hostess at his campus's guest residence. The job had three components: assisting the Holly Tree Inn and Annex's off-campus guests and resident faculty members, overseeing the schedules of its four full-time maids, and running the dining room. "I accepted the position at Hampton hoping that there would be a place for my husband and mother as well," Parks recalled, "but it didn't work out. They remained in Detroit." It shows how independent Rosa Parks had become that she would leave her husband in Detroit—where he was attending barber school to get his Michigan license—for a full year to work at the predominantly "Negro College" in the Tidewater region of Virginia.

It was an opportunity she could not pass up. The Hampton Normal and Agricultural Institute had been founded in 1868 by General Samuel Chapman Armstrong, the son of a Hawaiian missionary, as a coeducational school for African Americans. Armstrong had served as a lieutenant colonel commanding the Ninth U.S. Colored Troops Regiment during the Civil War, after which he became an agent of the Freedmen's Bureau, tasked with helping former slaves make the transition out of slavery. Armstrong built the college— which simplified its name to the Hampton Institute in 1930 and changed it to Hampton University in 1984—as a center for training future black leaders and teachers who would spread educational opportunities to the larger black population.

The three-story American colonial inn where Rosa worked, constructed in 1888, included on its first floor the office for the hostess, two small living rooms for informal entertainment, and the kitchen and faculty dining room. She soon found a favorite spot near the inn under the huge gnarled branches of the Emancipation Oak, in the shade of which the Virginia Peninsula's black community had gathered in 1863 to read Lincoln's famous address freeing America's slaves. Even more inspiring were the students at Hampton, all so smart and well mannered that they couldn't help but make her proud. Parks became particularly close to a Sioux student, and began reading up on Crazy Horse and the Red River War. And her pay was respectable, too; she could send money home every month to her husband, who had found a job as a combination instructor and maintenance man at his barber college in Detroit—and who for the first time in his life had registered to vote.

Reality came back into this idyll on September 17, 1958. With school just back in session for the fall semester, Parks was extremely busy that Saturday making sure every room at the Holy Tree Inn was equipped with clean sheets and hot water. Earlier that afternoon she had received a gift by special delivery from Martin Luther King, Jr.: a copy of his new book, *Stride Toward Freedom*, an autobiographical account of the Montgomery bus boycott. It was inscribed "To Rosa Parks: Whose creative witness was the great force that led to the modern stride toward freedom." She had scanned the text and had been elated to discover that King had written very highly of her, in her exuberance even showing the citation to the four maids she supervised. Then, just as she was settling into a chair in the inn's parlor to start reading the book in earnest, a news report came over the radio: King had been stabbed in the chest by a crazed female assailant at a book signing at Blumstein's department store in Harlem. Parks immediately dropped to her knees and prayed for his life. "I became hysterical and cried," she recalled. Others at Hampton telephoned Harlem Hospital, to which King had been rushed by ambulance, to learn his condition and other details of the assassination attempt by a forty-two-year-old paranoid schizophrenic named Izola Ware Curry. Doctors had removed two ribs and portions of King's breastbone in order to extract Curry's Japanese penknife from King's chest, which had grazed his aorta. "I was very relieved when the operation was successful and he was all right," Parks said. As she cried and prayed alone at the Hampton Institute, she realized just how much King meant to her people and how she had entrusted all her own aspirations to his care.

That Christmas, two years after she had set off the bus boycott that made King's name, Parks returned home to Detroit for the holidays and decided to stay. She loved the Holy Tree Inn and enjoyed Hampton's students and faculty, but her mother and husband were not holding up well in her absence. "I did inquire around Hampton to see if I could get housing for all of us and get my husband a job at the local barbershop for blacks, but I wasn't successful at either one," Parks recalled. She was sorry to leave the Hampton Institute; it was the only job she had ever had that put her in charge of other people, and she had proved a good manager. What's more, she would miss the milder climate, in which her arthritis bothered her so much less than the wind, sleet, and snow of the Great Lakes.

Returning from Virginia, Parks had little trouble finding a job: She was quickly hired full-time as a seamstress in Leonard and May Stockton's small shop in downtown Detroit and would spend the next five years, 1959–1964, working at the Stockton Sewing Company, a single-floor storefront crammed with sewing machines and ironing boards beneath a jungle of hand irons hanging from the ceiling. As she had in Montgomery to much greater consequence, Parks rode a city bus to work, often catching another home only after ten hours spent power-sewing cotton aprons and skirts by the hundreds. Paid about 75 cents for each piece completed, Parks was grateful for the grueling job and the steady income it provided to support her husband and mother.

It was during Parks's tenure at the Stockton Sewing

Company, in 1961, that she met new fellow worker Elaine Eason Steele, then a sixteen-year-old student at Cass Technical High School, just across the street. Steele was astonished to discover that the real-life Rosa Parks was her workmate, that the civil rights heroine of her history class was now sewing aprons in a tiny factory on the east side of Detroit. "She was so sweet and nice and showed me how to use the power-industrial Singer machine—how to place the garment under the needle just right," Steele marveled nearly forty years later.

Although they were generations apart, Parks and Steele soon discovered they had two important things in common: Both were Methodists, and both had been born in Tuskegee, Alabama. In fact, Steele's father, Frank Eason, had been one of the famed Tuskegee Airmen who served so nobly in the Second World War, after which he had moved his family north to Detroit. Fate had handed the proud, inquisitive Elaine Steele—who looked like the young Eartha Kitt—the chance to sew aprons next to the most celebrated woman in civil rights history. The curious teenager took full advantage of her good fortune, peppering Parks with questions: Was she still getting death threats in Detroit? What was Martin Luther King, Jr., really like? Had she ever met Harry Belafonte? "She was always very patient and calm," Steele recalled. "She would answer my questions, but when work had to be done, she would say in a gracious, motherly whisper: 'Maybe we can talk a little later.'" But Steele lasted only five days at the factory before being fired for low output. "I thought accuracy was more important than speed," she said, laughing. "Leonard Stockton didn't see it that way." Nevertheless, after Steele graduated from high school she stayed in touch with Parks, who embraced the young firebrand as if she were a daughter.

As had been the case in Montgomery, of course, her job was merely Parks's source of income—civil-rights activism remained her true vocation. The SCLC had adopted her as an honorary member, and she attended its conventions and retreats when she could. Although never involved in the SCLC's decision-making process, Parks brought a much-needed gentility to the group's often contentious gatherings. At the September 1962 SCLC convention in Birmingham, at which James Meredith's desegregation of the University of Mississippi occupied everybody's mind, her nurturing demeanor proved particularly helpful in the wake of another bizarre attack on King. As he closed the convention by recapping its proceedings and reminding the participants of upcoming fund-raisers in New York, a white man from the audience suddenly rushed the stage and punched the preacher in the face. Staggering backward, clearly dizzy from the initial blow, King refused to defend himself even as his assailant continued to hit him. A startled Septima Clark, along with Parks and the rest of the assemblage, marveled at the way King just dropped his hands "like a newborn baby" and stared calmly at his attacker. When several SCLC delegates jumped onto the stage to apprehend the man, King waved them away, shouting, "Don't touch him! We have to pray for him."

It was a frightening yet uplifting moment for Parks, who was sitting near the stage. "That, for many of us, was proof that Dr. King believed so completely in nonviolence that it was even stronger than his instinct to protect himself from attack," she said later. King kept talking softly to his assailant—who it would later be revealed was an American Nazi Party member angry that black entertainer Sammy Davis, Jr., had married a white woman—as he was led away. Parks immediately rushed backstage to attend to King, giving him two Bayer aspirins and a Coca-Cola—her remedy for headaches—and consoling him while he pressed an ice pack to his throbbing head. King refused to press charges, although Birmingham's chief of police, Eugene "Bull" Connor, did, from fear of bad press. Parks glowed decades later: "I was so proud of Dr. King. His restraint was more powerful than a hundred fists."

The next time the two heroes of the Montgomery bus boycott got together was on June 23, 1963, in Detroit, for what is known as King's Great March to Freedom. In a dress rehearsal for the upcoming March on Washington, King led a procession of thousands down Woodward Avenue to Cobo Hall, the downtown arena where the Detroit Pistons played basketball. Rosa Parks was at his side for most of the afternoon and thought his remarks commemorating the one hundredth anniversary of the Emancipation Proclamation the best she had ever heard. "He reminded everybody that segregation and discrimination were rampant in Michigan as well as Alabama," Parks recalled of the speech. He concluded with the soon-to-be-famous "I Have a Dream" incantation, offering the stirring promise that "right here in Detroit a Negro will be able to buy a house or rent a house anywhere that their money will carry them." When the local Motown Records—nicknamed "Hitsville USA" for producing million sellers by Stevie Wonder, Marvin Gaye, the Four Tops, the Miracles, and other musical acts—released a spoken-word album entitled *The Great March to Freedom*, a live recording of King's Cobo Hall speech, Parks played it regularly, wearing out the grooves. "It was like a shot of adrenaline," a friend recalled. "She listened to that record nonstop."

Parks met up with King again a few weeks later, at the historic March on Washington for Jobs and Freedom. On August 28, 1963, more than a quarter-million people gathered near the Lincoln Memorial under a cloudless blue sky for the greatest civil rights rally in U.S. history. Organized by A. Philip Randolph and Bayard Rustin, whose threat to lead a march on Washington against employment discrimination in 1941 had spurred FDR to create the Fair Employment Practices Commission, the event was essentially an outlet for African Americans to express their anger at white resistance to integration and to demonstrate black unity. The SCLC had invited Parks to participate, but shortly after arriving, she grew disenchanted with the sexism she encountered. It turned out that she and the other female civil rights leaders in attendance, including Septima Clark, Ella Baker, Daisy Bates, and Diane Nash Bevel, would not be allowed to march alongside the men, nor were any women invited to speak on the program. It was an outrage, considering the role women had already played in America's civil rights movement. "All I remember Rosa saying," Bates recalled, "is that our time will someday come."

Sensing their disappointment, Randolph hastily arranged for a "Tribute to Women" segment to be added, for which Parks and other prominent women leaders would be asked to stand and be recognized *pro forma*. It was an exercise in tokenism to Parks, who was more hurt than angered by the slight. She couldn't believe that she and Septima Clark were being treated like hostesses and was downright floored that dancer Josephine Baker, an international sensation who had flown in from France, was not even asked to speak. In fact, the only women granted access to the microphone were contralto Marian Anderson, for her rousing performance of "He's Got the Whole World in His Hands," and gospel singer Mahalia Jackson, whose rendition of "I Been 'Buked and I Been Scorned" brought down the house. Parks found the entire event, including King's soaring oratory, tainted by a male chauvinism every bit as ugly in its discrimination as Jim Crow. "Nowadays, women wouldn't stand for being kept so much in the background," she wrote in My Story, "but back then, women's rights hadn't become a popular cause yet." Upon returning to Detroit in 1963, however, Parks became more vocal for women's rights while paradoxically maintaining many old-school customs, such as always serving men their dinner first.

Despite its deep failings, the March on Washington—coupled with the assassination of President John F. Kennedy later in 1963—inspired Parks to take a more active part in Detroit's local politics. Early in 1964 she volunteered to work on the campaign of a little-known Democratic candidate for Michigan's First District seat in the U.S. House of Representatives: John Conyers, a thirty-five-year-old African-American attorney whose slogan was "Jobs, Justice, Peace." Conyers was a passionate civil rights advocate who had taken part in a voter-registration drive in Mississippi and attended the March on Washington. When Conyers, who had been a legislative aide to Representative John Vingelli, decided to run for Congress himself—a bold step back then for one so young and unknown, not to mention black—Parks offered her services at his campaign headquarters, where she was immediately put to work answering mail and meeting

young people. Even more valuable was her appeal on Conyers's behalf to Martin Luther King, Jr.

In an effort to stay out of the political crossfire, King had
always observed an ironclad rule: Never endorse any candidate for public office. But his resolve on this point crumbled
the instant Rosa Parks telephoned him and said, "You've just
got to come to Detroit and embrace Brother Conyers. We
need you." Unable to say no to the guiding angel of the
Montgomery bus boycott—with whom he would share the
September 1964 cover of *Ebony*—Dr. King traveled to Detroit that Easter weekend, delivered a rousing lecture at the
Central Methodist Church, and then endorsed Conyers's
long-shot bid for the House. "King's crucial statement on my
behalf quadrupled my visibility in the black community,"
Conyers testified. "Therefore, if it wasn't for Rosa Parks, I
never would have gotten elected." Six other Democrats—
two of them quite prominent in Detroit—were also vying for
the nomination, but Conyers eked out a victory in the primary by a whisker-thin margin of 128 votes. From there he
went on to clobber Highland Park's Republican mayor Bob
Blackwell in the general election and become a U.S. congressman. The first thing he did in the office was to hire Rosa
Parks.

After the election Parks quit her job at the Stockton
Sewing Company, and on March 1, 1965, she started working as a member of Representative Conyers's Detroit staff, in
a third-floor office in the Michigan State Building at the intersection of Woodward Avenue and West Grand Boulevard.
Much of her job involved the same functions she had performed in Alabama for the NAACP and E. D. Nixon: She
handled constituent cases, answered phones, met with visitors,

arranged the congressman's schedule, and pitched in on anything else that needed doing. As always, Parks proved a model employee: polite, punctual, diligent, and honest. Conyers had made a wise appointment indeed—one that would pay him considerable political dividends over the years, until Parks retired at age seventy-five on September 30, 1988. "Rosa Parks was so famous that people would come by my office to meet with her, not me," he explained. "It was incredible. She had correspondence and calls coming in, and she was traveling back and forth. She was a little embarrassed, humbly apologizing to me for having to leave. And I was saying, 'Rosa, you keep doing what you have to do. Don't worry about this job.'"

Of course, not all the response to her new employment was favorable. "We don't think John Conyers should be hiring a person of your low caliber, Rosa, to work in his office," began one letter she received at the congressman's office. "Maybe in his private home for purposes of scrubbing floors as a domestic maid, perhaps—but certainly not doing office work. You are far too much of a troublemaker and rabble-rouser. We cannot so soon forget all the chaos you made about 'going to the back of the bus.' As a matter of fact, you are to blame, gal, for the current revolution going on among niggers and whites today! You ought to hang that kinky ole head of yours in deep shame, gal, for what you did!" She was also sent rotten watermelons, "Die, wench" postcards, even a voodoo doll with toothpicks stuck in its vitals. Parks shrugged it off, even taking pride in the ire her Christian righteousness raised among vulgar bigots.

Thirty-five years later, Conyers could only laugh at the notion held in 1965 by many whites in Detroit—including

the press and the police—that Rosa Parks was an outside ag-
itator. "She was considered a dangerous person." Conyers
chuckled in retrospect. "People called her a troublemaker."
The evidence indicated quite the contrary: Conyers was fas-
cinated by Parks's gentleness and amazed that she and the
icon of the American civil rights movement were one and
the same. Yet he couldn't deny that Parks had an aura of
something akin to majesty, without the arrogance. And even
he found it difficult to coax her into easy banter. "It was a little bit confounding," Conyers admitted, "because you
wanted to say, 'Take your shoes off, relax, have a drink with
the boys, go dancing,' or something like that. But that wasn't
Rosa. She was like a nun." What struck Conyers the most
was that Parks apparently had no temper. She never raised
her voice or betrayed anger in any way. "It was bizarre," he
said. "She never got in an argument, yet controversy was always swirling around her. You could never get her to say a
bad word about anybody—not even an obvious fool. She just
couldn't be negative. The discongruity was this: She had a
heavy progressive streak about her that was uncharacteristic
for a neat, religious, demure, churchgoing lady."

And that she certainly was. Throughout her years in Detroit, Rosa Parks was an active and devoted member of the
St. Matthew AME Church, located at 9746 Petoskey Road
in an old synagogue built to hold three hundred congregants
on two levels—men worshiping on the main floor and
women from the balcony. Tucked into one of Detroit's many
Polish neighborhoods, little St. Matthew's opened its hearts
and arms to Rosa Parks. Every Sunday, almost without ex-
ception from 1959 to 1964, she served as a church stewardess, her main function to assist in the rituals of baptism

and the Lord's Supper. In 1965, at the behest of Pastor Harold Huggins, Parks was elevated to deaconess, the highest office a woman in the AME church could hold short of being ordained as a minister. Once a deaconess, Parks's duties expanded to include fostering and promoting the general interests of the church, soliciting the friendship and sympathy of the general public, cheering the downcast, feeding the hungry, clothing the naked, sheltering the homeless, and saving the lost by visiting them in mental hospitals and prisons. It was a tall order clearly spelled out in the AME handbook, and Parks threw her all into filling it.

At first, Huggins was shocked that the great Rosa Parks—wearing an immaculately pressed dress-length deaconess uniform with a black bonnet, or skullcap, tied under the chin with a white ribbon—would attend such a small church as St. Matthew's, which had only two hundred members. There were twenty grander AME churches in Detroit that would have rolled out the red carpet for her. Yet she chose St. Matthew's, and for a simple reason: That was where her first cousin, Annie Mae Cruse, prayed. Her performance as deaconess was equally self-effacing; beyond appearing in her white or black uniform every Sunday, she prayed regularly on weekdays and helped print the church bulletin, saving nearly every program from the St. Matthew's services she attended, all of which can be found among her Wayne State papers. Occasionally, gawkers would turn up at the church to catch a peek of the "Mother of the Civil Rights Movement," but nothing unpleasant occurred in connection with her presence there; in fact, preachers came and went at St. Matthew's, but Rosa Parks remained a quiet constant. When the Reverend Eddie Robinson took over as pastor in 1966, he wasn't sure what to expect but maintained that "she taught me humility" in the end. "It was the most remarkable thing," Robinson said: "Fame hadn't touched her. She was still utter simplicity and utter humility."

Well, maybe, and only in part. It is simplistic to regard Parks as *Time* magazine did in its "Person of the Century" issue of December 31, 1999, lumping her in with Martin Luther King, Jr., as one of Mohandas K. Gandhi's "children" devoted to nonviolent resistance. Unlike Gandhi and King, Parks refused to rule out the righteous use of force. She believed that some wars were indeed just, that an abused person had the right to hit back, and that the ancient Hindu ideal of *ahimsa* Gandhi preached of, nonviolence toward all living things, did not apply to the starving or oppressed. She may have admired the Dr. King who allowed a misguided neo-Nazi to pummel him in Birmingham, but she thrilled to the one who thundered that the white power structure must give in to the SCLC's demands for voting rights or face a firestorm of black protests no one would be able to control. The slogan "Black Power" never snarled from Rosa Parks's lips, but she believed in it wholeheartedly. By the turbulent mid-1960s, the gentle Christian woman had become a tough-minded, free-thinking feminist who had grown impatient with gradualist approaches.

Yet because of her reputation as a mild Christian woman, historical accounts of Rosa Parks tend to overlook her quasi-militant side, including her admiration for Malcolm X, a black Nation of Islam member originally from Detroit. All the young boys who hung around the Parkses' Virginia Park apartment, to which they had moved in 1961, were enthralled with "Detroit Red," as the former Malcolm Little had been known in prison. Parks read everything she could find on Brother Malcolm's ministry and applauded his stance against alcohol and drugs. While she never approved of Malcolm X's virulent hatred of whites, his message of black self-sufficiency appealed to her immensely. "I had a lot of admiration for him, considering his background and where he came from and his having had to struggle so hard just to reach the point of being respected as a leader of the Black Muslims," Parks explained. "He was a very brilliant man."

It was Malcolm X's March 1964 pilgrimage to Mecca, which led him to quit the Nation of Islam and develop a less bigoted view of whites, that brought Rosa Parks closer to him intellectually. She read with great interest about his establishment of a Muslim mosque in Harlem and the Organization of Afro-American Unity and how, as an orthodox Muslim, he now condemned Nation of Islam leader Elijah Mohammed as a "racist" and "religious faker," charges so infuriating to the sect that its official newspaper pronounced Malcolm X "worthy of death." A week before he was assassinated, on February 21, 1965, Parks was invited to sit in the front row at a speech he gave in Detroit. "He spoke one Sunday evening and was shot the next," she lamented. She had met with Malcolm X privately during his Detroit visit and found him warm and engaging. Tall, articulate, bow-tied, and noticeably polite, he had made no denunciations of "white devils"; in fact, the new Malcolm X she encountered proselytized only about the equality of all races. The program he autographed for her that Sunday became a prized possession, and his black nationalist philosophy was one she would embrace as the civil rights struggle intensified through the late

1960s. "Dr. King used to say that black people should receive brutality with love, and I believed that this was a goal to work for," Parks explained, "but I couldn't reach that point in my mind at all. . . . Malcolm wasn't a supporter of nonviolence, either."

Chapter 11

Months of Bloody Sundays

EXACTLY A MONTH after Malcolm X was murdered, just a few weeks after she joined the Detroit staff of U.S. congressman John Conyers, Parks found herself drawn back to Montgomery once again. Two weeks earlier, on March 7, 1965, hundreds of African Americans had set out to march from Selma to the Alabama state capitol in Montgomery to demand federal protection of blacks' right to vote. As the peaceful throng proceeded onto the Edmund Pettus Bridge that spanned the Alabama River, however, the marchers were brutally assaulted by Selma city police and Alabama state troopers, most of them wearing gas masks.

Rosa Parks was at home in Detroit watching the ABC television premiere of *Judgment at Nuremberg*, Stanley Kramer's 1961 movie about Nazi war-crime trials, when the broadcast was suddenly interrupted by a live report from Selma. The shocking footage showed mounted policemen throwing tear-gas bombs and swinging billy clubs and electric cattle prods at friends of hers, including the Reverend Hosea Williams of the SCLC and John Lewis of SNCC. Alabama had turned into a war zone. Parks listened intently and cringed when she heard Dallas County sheriff Jim Clark shout, "Get those goddamned niggers! And get those goddamned white niggers."

No past incident had prepared Alabama governor George Wallace—a staunch segregationist—for the national media's scathing attacks on him after the barbarity on the Pettus Bridge. "George Wallace . . . has written another shameful page in his own record in the history of Alabama," began a typical *New York Times* editorial on March 8. Sympathy marches were quickly organized throughout America, including in Detroit, where Parks strode down Woodward Avenue in solidarity with her bleeding colleagues in Selma. She also consulted with her new boss, Representative Conyers, before the Michigan freshman met with Vice President Hubert H. Humphrey on March 12 to urge that the Alabama National Guard be activated to prevent any further violence. Conyers's Michigan colleague in the U.S. House, then Republican Gerald Ford, was equally outraged and announced that new legislation would use the "maximum power of the federal government to prevent further violence and to protect constitutional rights in Selma, Alabama."

Twenty years had passed since Parks had finally succeeded in registering to vote in Alabama, but the unofficial exclusion of African Americans from the polls had continued. Now the scenes from Selma drove Parks to despair that tyrannical officers of the law were still using the bludgeon to keep blacks from exercising their constitutional right to vote. So when Martin Luther King, Jr.—who had been in Atlanta on what was already being called "Bloody Sunday"—telephoned Parks about returning to Alabama to take part in another mass march to Montgomery, her answer was immediate: "Why, of course."

Since her bank account was virtually empty, Parks appealed to the United Automobile Workers, through her friend and manager Louise Tappes, owner of House of Beauty Hair Salon, whose husband, Sheldon, worked for the union, to pay her airfare from Detroit to Atlanta, and the union agreed to help. What's more, two UAW officials accompanied her the whole way, taking the same flight into Hartsfield Airport, riding the same chartered bus for the full two-hour trip to Montgomery, and checking her into the Ben Moore Hotel. The returning homegirl hugged her dear Montgomery friends Bertha Butler and Johnnie Mae Carr until all three were breathless, then shed her winter clothes for a cool cotton dress lent her by Carr. Parks was astonished to see how little Montgomery had changed in the eight years she had been away. "One of the first things I did was look at the buses," she said. "And yep—they were integrated. . . . That felt good."

After breakfast at Butler's home, Parks was driven to the City of St. Jude, a sprawling Roman Catholic church, school, and hospital complex built after the Great Depression and designed to serve everyone regardless of race, creed, gender, or socioeconomic status. This civic-minded compound on Montgomery's west side was the brainchlid of a visionary Irish-Catholic priest from Union City, New Jersey—Father Harold Purcell, at that time nationally known as the editor of *The Sign*, one of the nation's most popular family magazines. Purcell's dream had been to create an oasis of well-kept grounds scattered with serene religious statuary right in the middle of the squalid slums of black west Montgomery; the wonder is that he realized it, somehow managing to raise enough funds to construct a sturdy brick combination school, medical clinic, and social center on the outskirts of town.

By 1947, the resultant St. Jude Educational Institute enrolled some five hundred elementary and high school students and more than six hundred World War II veterans in its night school alone. The $1.5 million Purcell had collected for a general hospital afforded a facility with bed space for 162 patients and the most modern medical equipment available in the area. It seemed no less than a miracle: Montgomery's African Americans found themselves with one of the best hospitals in the South—and the only integrated one in the city—from which no one was turned away for lack of the means to pay for care. In addition, at the center of the compound, Purcell's moxie had enabled the erection of a magnificent cathedral, complete with a crucifix carved from Italy's finest Carrara marble and a soaring, blue-tiled roof that could be seen from miles away—all built by black labor. "It took me by surprise to see a white man stand up and defend black people," remembered E. D. Nixon, who had had various dealings with Father Purcell over the years. "It made a whole lot of people begin to see the light."

On March 25, 1965, Rosa Parks was greeted at the City of St. Jude by Father Paul Mullaney—who was Purcell's successor—a handsome, middle-aged priest from Pennsylvania who had made the bold decision to allow the thousands of marchers from Selma to spend the night on the Catholic compound's thirty-eight-acre grounds. With permission from the bishop in Mobile, Mullaney erected a tent city to house the marchers and hired a maintenance crew to be on a four-hour duty. The exhausted protesters—who had requested and received a court order allowing them to proceed along U.S. Highway 80 without interference—had walked forty-six miles in the three days since they had left Brown's chapel in Selma on Sunday, arriving at the City of St. Jude on

Wednesday evening with aching feet but soaring spirits: They had only four more miles to go. As soon as Parks arrived, she was swarmed by smiling old friends, except King, who to Parks seemed "distracted" and "unusually shy." The night before, more than ten thousand people had turned up and been treated to performances by top entertainers participating in the march, including Harry Belafonte, Joan Baez, Peter, Paul, and Mary, Sammy Davis, Jr., and Johnny Mathis. To many, Parks was a celebrity of equal magnitude.

For all the warmth of her welcome by the older generation, however, it seemed that many of the younger marchers had never heard of Rosa Parks. In fact, she drew so little notice from march organizers that she was shunted aside at a rally at the St. Jude athletic field before the final leg of the protest began. Overall, "being on the march was a strange experience," Parks recalled. "It seemed like such a short time that I had been out of Alabama, but so many young people had grown up in that time. They didn't know who I was and couldn't care less about me because they didn't know me."

As the demonstration progressed, Parks grew frustrated at her odd situation. No one had thought to give her one of the special colored jackets denoting "official" participants, so march organizers as well as the police kept making her stand off to the side. Happily, most of the time somebody from the earlier days of the civil-rights movement would see her standing alone and would either grab her hand and say, "Come march with me, Rosa," or approach her shyly and entreat, "Please, Mrs. Parks, march with me." For a while she linked arms with the great Alabama-bred folksinger Odetta, but before long they got separated in the crush of the crowd. After that, comedian Dick Gregory spotted her, and they walked together, laughing nervously about the number of police and federal troops on hand, until another authority figure noticed her lack of the right color jacket and made her leave the procession yet again. Over the course of the day she was sent to the sidelines four or five times.

Even from the fringes, however, as the marchers made their way up broad, tree-lined Dexter Avenue, Parks was awed by the sight of some twenty-five thousand people, most of them black, swarming around the state capitol waiting to hear Dr. King preach on voting rights. Fortunately, an SCLC veteran seized her arm and pulled her into the front ranks to cover the last quarter mile from Court Square to the capitol alongside Martin and Coretta King, Ralph and Juanita Abernathy, Ambassador Ralph Bunche, and the Reverend L. V. Reese.

Although federal judge Frank Johnson had ordered Governor Wallace to refrain from "harassing or threatening" the protesters, they were nevertheless met near the capitol by a horde of angry whites, many of whom recognized Parks and began jeering, "You're the culprit, Rosa," and "You'll get yours, Rosa Parks." Although the moment clearly belonged to King, Parks was also asked to address the crowd. Her soft voice barely audible over the crackling speakers, Parks spoke about the Highlander Folk School and what she learned there. "Most of my brief remarks explained that the propaganda being circulated to the crowd and displayed on a billboard outside Montgomery about Dr. King being a Communist was untrue," she said later. "The billboard showed a group of people at the Highlander Folk School pictured with the founder, Myles Horton, and indicated that the school supported communism. . . . Dr. King was never a student there, as the antagonists indicated. He was the keynote speaker at its twenty-fifth anniversary program."

And he outdid that oration on the afternoon of March 21, 1965, with one of the greatest speeches he would ever deliver, telling the throng: "We are on the move, and no wave of racism will stop us!" That evening, Martin and Coretta King flew back to Atlanta in grand spirits: the Selma-to-Montgomery march had been an unqualified success and was covered by the three television networks, the *New York Times*, and other major media outlets as if it were a defining moment in American history—which it was. Best of all, no one had been seriously injured during the protest.

Yet Rosa Parks, who took a bus back to Atlanta the next day, spent that evening scared and depressed at a segregated downtown hotel. "I remember feeling that something was not right," she explained. "Even though the march was over, I felt that everything was not right." All that night long she tossed and turned between insomnia and nightmares. In one dream, she was standing with Raymond next to a billboard in an open field when a white man in Levi's overalls suddenly appeared with a shotgun in hand and aimed it at her. She woke up in a sweat and turned on the eleven o'clock news to learn that Viola Liuzzo, a thirty-nine-year-old white housewife and mother from Detroit, had been murdered on a lonely stretch of road in neighboring Lowndes County while shuttling marchers back and forth to the site of the Montgomery protest.

Like Parks, Liuzzo had not come to Alabama to cause trouble or make headlines. She had also watched Bloody Sunday unfold on television, been horrified by the sight of state troopers cracking open the skulls of peaceful demonstrators on the Edmund Pettus Bridge, and decided, in spite of her husband's pleas, to drive by herself to Dixie and to offer rides to any Selma-to-Montgomery marchers who needed them. For this she had been shot in the head twice at close range with a .38-caliber pistol: the crime of being a white woman with a black passenger in her car.

Back in Detroit, a distraught Parks went to the funeral home to view Viola's open casket and attended a memorial service at which she extended her condolences to Viola's five grieving children. After that, Parks monitored the Liuzzo murder trial closely from Conyers's office. "The defense lawyers for the three indicted Klansmen did everything in their power to discredit Mrs. Liuzzo's character," Parks would write in a foreword to Beatrice Siegel's book *Murder on the Highway: The Viola Liuzzo Story*. "They accused her of being a Communist, a radical, and morally irresponsible. . . . Though the Klansmen were not convicted of murder, they were put in jail for ten years for violating Mrs. Liuzzo's civil rights. The verdict was a surprise to many people, especially civil rights workers. We were not accustomed to Klansmen being sentenced for anything, so a conviction was a step in the right direction."

Many friends of the still shy and self-effacing Rosa Parks maintained that the vicious murder of Viola Liuzzo mortified her, while simultaneously toughening her resolve to fight political injustice at any cost. She became much more active in the Women's Public Affairs Committee of 1,000, a multiracial organization dedicated to improving relations among the races. On April 3, 1965, Parks eagerly accepted the group's invitation to join Ralph Abernathy and Coretta King as a guest speaker at a tribute dinner held at Detroit's Cobo Hall, and she made a passionate speech, through tears of grief, about the death of Viola Liuzzo. "This was no time to be dormant," Parks claimed. "We were finally getting to President Lyndon Johnson, we were finally making it clear that voting rights weren't negotiable."

In the wake of what happened in Selma, Parks also increased her public appearances on behalf of the SCLC and NAACP and accepted honorary lifetime membership in the National Association of Colored Women. She was on hand when President Johnson signed his historic civil rights legislation. By this time, however, her traditional integrationist posture had embraced elements of the "Black Power" movement's more militant attitude. She also began wearing colorful African-inspired garb on occasion, attending performances at the Concept East Theater, the first African-American theater company in the urban North, and listening to WCHB, the nation's first major black-owned-and-operated radio station. Around this time Parks befriended Motown Records founder Berry Gordy, Jr., whose Black Forum label produced spoken-word albums by African Americans. She also started making appearances at rallies sponsored by Detroit's Freedom Now Party, formed in 1963, as the first all-black political party in America led by outspoken activists opposed to the gradual approach to securing equal rights.

Never, of course, did Rosa Parks condone senseless violence in the quest for those rights or for any other reason. It sickened her to see Detroit's image as a model city for race relations shattered on July 23, 1967, when it exploded into what would become eight days of rioting, vandalism, and brutality in one of the most destructive civil disorders in American history. "What triggered the riot in my opinion, to a considerable extent, was that between urban renewal and expressways, poor black people were bulldozed out of their homes," Michigan governor George W. Romney later lamented. "They had no place to go in the suburbs because of suburban restrictions."

The trouble began close to four o'clock that midsummer morning, after the Detroit police raided an illegal after-hours spot—known in the black community as a "blind pig"—on Twelfth Street. A mob quickly formed outside the club, and soon the city's long-simmering racial tensions erupted. First a few bottles and cans were tossed at the police; then the ugliness escalated into looting and arson punctuated by random gunfire. The mayor soon asked Governor Romney—a leading contender for the 1968 Republican presidential nomination—to activate the state's National Guard as the massive riots continued. In the end it took nearly five thousand regular U.S. Army troops until July 30 to restore order. The disturbances exacted a staggering toll: some 5,000 people left homeless, 7,231 arrested, more than 700 seriously injured, 43 dead, and $50 million in property damage. The racial violence hit Rosa Parks close to home: Her husband's barbershop had been among the many small businesses looted. All of his haircutting equipment was stolen, their new car had been vandalized, and good friends had been badly beaten.

Montgomery during the bus boycott had produced some frightening moments, but Parks had never witnessed anything remotely like the terror and chaos in Detroit. To her mind, what occurred had nothing to do with civil rights—it was pure hooliganism, and she had little sympathy for its perpetrators, whom she deemed "thieves." As she would lament of later riots in an interview in the August 1971 issue of

Ebony, it harmed the cause when looting and burning were passed off as being "in the name of civil rights."

As appalled as Parks had been at the events of July 1967, they paled next to the cruel jolt the whole world suffered on April 4, 1968—the day Martin Luther King, Jr., was assassinated on a balcony outside his room at the Lorraine Motel in Memphis. Parks had last heard King speak at the 1967 SCLC Convention, where he had questioned the morality of capitalism's narrow distribution of wealth. "The movement," King had said then, "must address itself to the question of restructuring the whole of American society." It thrilled her as much as his denunciation of the Vietnam War in New York earlier that year. Parks was listening to the radio with her mother, Leona McCauley, when the regular broadcast was interrupted by the bulletin that Dr. King had been shot in the head, followed by another report that the shot had been fatal. "Mama and I wept quietly together," Parks said simply. "I was deeply grieved."

During the Montgomery bus boycott, Septima Clark had said more than once that chaos inspired creative thinking and thus should be welcomed. But early in April 1968, Parks couldn't avoid feeling that what had been healthy chaos in the 1950s had soured into destructive anarchy in the 1960s, marked by race riots and anti–Vietnam War protests that left ghettos burning, college campuses seething, and John F. Kennedy, Malcolm X, and Martin Luther King, Jr., dead. As dissatisfaction built into bitter anger among African Americans, Parks worried that assault and arson were replacing Gandhian nonviolence as the means of social protest. Desperate to stop this trend, she packed her tattered blue suitcase and arranged to head immediately with her friend

Louise Tappes to help continue the peaceful march King had been leading to support Memphis's garbage workers' strike. Raymond Parks thought she had gone mad, but he had long ago given up trying to dissuade his stubborn wife with concerns about her personal safety. As she waited for her ride to the airport, she played Sam Cooke's record "Long Time Comin'," which begins: "I was born by the river in a little old tent, and just like the river I've been running ever since. It's been a long time comin' but I know change is goin' to come." She later credited that gorgeous pop ballad with saving her sanity. "His smooth voice was like medicine to the soul," she recalled. "It was as if Dr. King was speaking directly to me."

A part of Rosa Parks died with King that day. She sobbed uncontrollably even while praying to God, read Psalms 27 out loud in a futile effort to stanch her tears, then walked out her front door, overwhelmed with grief: She had loved Dr. King; now he was lost to the Promised Land while she was in bumper-to-bumper traffic and on her way to Memphis with her mind reeling that her legacy would be forever linked in history to his. She was too numb to feel anger, only the sharp loneliness of knowing that her circle had contracted inward, and with it her spirit. "I was lost," she said. "How else can I describe it?"

When she got to Memphis, she composed herself enough to speak with many of the striking garbage workers, but their despair made Parks realize that the only marching to do now was in the funeral procession for their fallen hero. The entire civil rights movement was paralyzed with grief and confusion over what to do next. Parks was grateful when, after only a few hours in town, singer Harry Belafonte offered her a ride to Atlanta in his private plane to attend King's funeral.

There she met briefly with Democratic presidential candidate Robert F. Kennedy and thanked him for the wrenching speech he had given in an Indianapolis ghetto upon hearing of King's assassination. Shortly after King's funeral, Parks had another premonition in a nightmare, this time that Robert F. Kennedy—whom she fiercely admired—would be killed; two months later, he was. "It just seemed like we were losing everybody we thought was good," Parks recalled. She felt an aching emptiness with the realization that America's civil rights era was over.

CHAPTER 12

Onward

MARTIN LUTHER KING, JR., didn't start the American civil rights movement, but early on his brilliance made him its polestar, and when that guiding light was blotted out in April 1968, those who had looked to it seemed to lose their way in the darkness his death left behind. Most civil rights organizations, including the SCLC that was dear to Rosa Parks, drifted into irrelevance. Although she herself continued to put her all toward John Conyers's efforts in the U.S. Congress, attended NAACP functions, and diligently went about her deaconess duties at St. Matthew AME, Parks's image became more symbolic and less activist. Many whites in Montgomery were embarrassed by the boycott legacy and blamed Parks. Some blacks were jealous and thought their personal roles were equally or more historically important than Rosa Parks's so-called grandstand act. Others—such as Montgomery city councilman Luther Oliver—annointed her "Saint Rosa" and spearheaded an effort to raise fifty thousand dollars to help support her as the years drew on. Yet no one seemed to care anymore how she viewed the state of American society, or why she so ardently backed Democrat George McGovern's candidacy for president in 1972, or what she thought about anything else. The few scholars and reporters who did seek Parks out, primarily during

Black History month, wanted to know only one thing: why she had refused to give up her seat on that fateful bus on December 1, 1955.

It proved a bittersweet homecoming when Parks returned to Montgomery at the invitation of city officials in December 1975 to celebrate the twentieth anniversary of the bus boycott. The theme of the city's commemorative conference was "The Struggle Continues," and the idea behind it was to give congressmen, clergymen, activists, businessmen, students, and the rest of the community an opportunity to assess what the civil rights movement had accomplished, and what remained to be done.

Conference coordinator Leon Hall had been just eight years old when Parks had refused to budge. "The big difference made by the boycott," he told the press two decades later, "was that black men and women across this nation are now standing with their backs straight." The evidence supported his claim. When Parks was arrested in 1955, Alabamans had elected not a single black official; in 1975 the state had 200 African-American officeholders, including 13 of the 108 members of its lower house and 2 of its 36 state senators. Whereas fewer than 100 blacks had held public office across the entire South on the Bloody Sunday of March 1965, ten years later upwards of 1,700 did, and more than a million and a half Southern blacks had joined the voter rolls. In the North, in 1968 Shirley Chisholm had become the first black woman elected to the U.S. Congress, and across the country major cities had voted in African American mayors, including Coleman Young in Detroit, Tom Bradley in Los Angeles, and Maynard Jackson in Atlanta.

These advances still were not enough for Rosa Parks.

Speaking from the pulpit at the Holt Street Baptist Church in 1975, in a voice sounding more forceful at age sixty-two than it had ever sounded before, she urged the mostly black crowd to seek even more offices. "Don't stop," she implored. "Keep on. Keep on keeping on."

But her own advice was getting ever harder to take as health problems mounted for both Rosa and Raymond Parks throughout the 1970s. The stomach ulcers she had developed in Montgomery continued to plague her, and she began suffering heart trouble as well. On two occasions a few years apart she fell on the ice in Detroit, the first time breaking her ankle, the second her wrist. Meanwhile the family members closest to Rosa—her mother, Leona, brother, Sylvester, and husband, Raymond—had all developed cancer. "Mama continues to be quite ill," she wrote Virginia Durr on April 3, 1977. "She is still in the hospital, but not improving either mentally or physically. The doctor hopes she will eat more and gain some strength before going home. Parks is keeping up very well and I'm doing my best to keep going." She went on in the letter to lament her detachment from the civil rights circuit. "Fannie Lou Hamer was dead quite a while before I knew of it. I was not getting the news by TV or radio or newspaper. No one mentioned it to me. It was sad news." Raymond Parks's ailments were far more grave, and after a five-year struggle with throat cancer he died in 1977 at age seventy-four.

Although he had never been a financial success, his ambitions hindered by racism and heavy drinking, Raymond Parks had been a loyal husband of the rare sort who supported his household and didn't object to his mother-in-law's living in his home. He was, in fact, a source of strength for

Rosa Parks in many ways others didn't understand. Despite his constant terror that his wife was going to get herself killed by some crazy white bigot, he never tried to stop her, be it from attending a civil rights rally across the street or flying a thousand miles to march with Dr. King. He always respected her, and for that she loved him unconditionally. When her husband's stainless-steel casket was lowered into the ground at Detroit's Woodlawn Cemetery, Parks felt an unfillable void open within her, one that would yawn wider only three months later, when her baby brother and only sibling, Sylvester, succumbed to stomach cancer, leaving thirteen children behind. "Words can't explain the double loss I felt," Parks whispered. "It was a sad, sorrowful time. My mother was also dying with cancer, and for a while I was traveling to three different hospitals a day."

With her husband gone, Parks faced a critical dilemma at home: Who would take care of her mother while she was at work? Unable to afford a nurse, she decided to place Leona McCauley in the Eventide nursing home, which was near enough to her job in downtown Detroit that she could visit her mother three times a day. When this arrangement quickly proved too exhausting, Parks packed up her home on Virginia Park, rented an apartment at the Bi-Centennial Towers on Alexandrine Street, a high-rise designed specifically for senior citizens, and moved her mother out of the nursing home and into the apartment with her. "We lived together there until 1979," Parks said. "She was ninety-one when she died, and I found myself all alone."

It was in those painful circumstances that Elaine Eason Steele became, for all intents and purposes, the daughter Rosa Parks never had as well as her best friend and personal manager. Their relationship had changed and matured as the two women did. At the time of King's assassination, Steele was a member of the Republic of New Africa, a radical organization whose mission was to have an American state—perhaps Alabama or Mississippi—governed exclusively by black people. This separatist position was adopted by a few mainstream civil rights figures, including James Forman and James Meredith. Although she remained a Christian, Steele had grown frustrated with her local Christian Methodist Church's refusal to recognize what she believed was a historical fact: that Jesus Christ had been black. But in the course of spending time with the motherly Parks the feisty Steele mellowed, and by 1972 her New African nationalism had been supplanted by Christian universalism. "I learned through Mrs. Parks not to have animosity or hate or be judgmental," Steele explained. Their friendship solidified during their commutes together— Parks usually driving them in her white Chevrolet station wagon—to and from their jobs at Detroit's downtown federal building, where Parks worked for John Conyers and Steele was employed in the offices of the U.S. district court. Before long the pair became inseparable, spending their free time together working nonstop on community and civil rights activities.

"Elaine had grown so close to Mrs. Parks," Steele's sister, Anita Peek, recalled, "that she even felt her pain." The strong-willed Steele, a mother of two, soon made herself an iron drawbridge between Parks and journalists or any other visitors who wanted a word with the aging icon. She scheduled her bookings, accompanied her on appearances, and no longer let people take advantage of her "sweet spirit." Over the years, however, Parks's nephews and nieces would express some bitterness at the protective way Steele lorded over their aunt's affairs, while the *Detroit News* published a stream of unfavorable articles about her attempts to market the legend. Steele, however, maintained that her only motive was to help her heroine avoid bankruptcy and exhaustion from accepting every request to attend something, invariably for free.

In truth, until Steele took charge, Parks had dutifully been answering every one of the thousands of letters she received each year from around the world, not wanting to be discourteous to her admirers. Parks was racked by ulcers and fatigue, and her eyesight had also been damaged from years of flashbulbs going off in her face—no longer so much a problem from the press as from fans eager for photographic proof of their brush with greatness. Often at Conyers's office, for example, Parks would be set upon by camera-wielding schoolchildren as if she were some roadside attraction on their field trips, and it was Elaine Eason Steele who put an end to these impromptu photo sessions. In 1987, when Parks was involved in a terrible automobile accident, it was Steele who kept the reporters at bay, and the next year, when Parks had a pacemaker implanted in her chest to correct an irregular heartbeat, it was Steele who determined that she had to turn down nearly all speaking requests. Steele also arranged for Parks to winter in Los Angeles as a houseguest of famed civil rights lawyer Leo Branton and his wife, Geraldine, a ritual she repeated for twelve straight years. She particularly loved the family setting and morning conversations on human rights with Geraldine. "The California sunshine beats shoveling snow," Rosa joked to a reporter from the *Los Angeles Times*. "But my heart is always in Michigan." When

Parks's other closest friend, Louise Tappes, died in 1989, Steele's role expanded to include accompanying Parks on trips back and forth across the country to receive honorary doctorates, attend award dinners, and the like.

As their relationship deepened, Steele's primary aim became simply to help establish a lasting monument to Parks's legacy in line with philosopher Cornel West's belief that "every day is borrowed time. You want to be able to use life as well as death as a form of service to something bigger than you; that makes life meaningful." Thus, it was with an eye toward posterity that the two women created the Rosa and Raymond Parks Institute for Self-Development in 1987. As youth leader of the NAACP's Montgomery branch, Rosa, with Raymond's support, had tried to motivate youngsters to reach their highest potential. Likewise, the Detroit institute's mission would be to teach underprivileged youngsters aged eleven to seventeen how to conduct themselves with dignity and honor in the modern world. They would do so through programs advocating the philosophy of "quiet strength" in the training of future leaders. "This institute is my lifelong dream," Parks would say. "I just love the young people; they're our angels of the future."

The national headquarters of the Parks Institute occupied a modern office suite in downtown Detroit's Cadillac Square. But the soul of the nonprofit organization resided in Parks's rented house, a two-story redbrick colonial with black latticework around the windows located at 9336 Wildemere, just a mile from St. Matthew AME. There was a grassroots, community-center feel to the office part of the residence that Parks shared with Ossie Jefferson Corley, a registered nurse committed to the holistic heath care movement. Their home often bustled like a campaign headquarters: John Coltrane and Ella Fitzgerald jazzed from a tiny radio as volunteers paraded to and from the large pigeonhole mailbox placed out front to collect Parks's mail, their unwiped boots soiling the shaggy tan carpet beneath a bulletin board splattered with snapshots and announcements. Hung prominently on the wall was a photocopied sign reading: "When We Feel the Stress and the Storm We Learn the Strength of the Anchor." And everyone knew who that anchor was.

Parks and Steele decided to model their institute's main effort after the Michigan Coalition of Human Rights program "The Freedom Ride," which took Detroit-area students to visit important civil rights sites. In 1988 the two women joined the students on a historical journey to Selma, Montgomery, and Lowndes County, Alabama. The following year the institute started the "Reverse Freedom Tour," where students from the South came north tracing the Underground Railroad. In other words, youngsters would study African-American history with the mother of the civil rights movement as their freedom guide. "We didn't know if we should clap or bow when we first met her," said 1996 tour participant Nathaniel Phillips of Detroit, summing up the experience for most graduates. "The trip changed the way I carry myself. There was so much talent, intelligence, and enthusiasm in the group."

Parks had a genuine passion to make young people interested in history, and she realized she was in a unique position to do so. Thus, she decided to personally escort the students in her institute's "Pathways to Freedom" program, many of whom had never been out of urban ghettos before. Every year a different focus was selected for students to conduct field research: to the Great Plains to see where the Buffalo Soldiers had fought; to Oklahoma to study Andrew Jackson's "Trail of Tears"; to Harpers Ferry to remember John Brown's rebellion; and to Nova Scotia to begin learning about the program's primary focus, the Underground Railroad, along with memorizing the biography of its most famous conductor, Harriet Tubman. With Canada—the Railroad's terminus—just across the Detroit River, the institute's location was ideal for illuminating the story of the coordinated network of abolitionists who before the Civil War had brought tens of thousands of slaves out of their shackles in the Deep South along a secret route dotted with wooded hideouts and safe houses to freedom in the North.

Youth from around the nation signed up for the institute's monthlong summer "freedom rides" to historic sites, even though TV, radio, and video games were forbidden and journal keeping and oral reports were required. Along the way Parks, a converted vegetarian, also talked to the teenagers about nutrition as well as about personal responsibility, and encouraged them to continue sharing their experiences by writing to each other after the tour ended. Between 1987 and 2000 more than five thousand young people took part in programs at the Rosa and Raymond Parks Institute for Self-Development. "I'm hoping that we'll reach as many young people as we can," Parks said, "and that they will be motivated, trained, and inspired to reach their highest potential in life."

The desperate need for such efforts was underscored with a slash on August 30, 1994, when a young Detroit delinquent named Joseph Skipper brutally attacked Rosa Parks in her own bedroom for pocket money. The bizarre incident occurred at eight o'clock in the evening, as Parks was preparing to turn in by switching on the fans in her tiny second-floor bedroom. Suddenly she heard a loud thud from below, followed by an agitated male voice calling out. She crept downstairs in her bathrobe to investigate, and was startled by a whiskey-soaked black man in his twenties claiming that he had chased away an intruder who had broken through the back door. Only a heart as pure as Parks's could have found the story plausible. "He wanted to protect me, is what he said," she related. "And he wanted me to give him some money."

The actual intruder suggested a tip of three or four dollars for having chased away the imaginary burglar, and Parks, anxious to get rid of him, asked him to wait while she went upstairs to get some money. It was a painfully innocent mistake. The man followed her to the bedroom, and when she picked up her handbag he turned menacing and demanded *all* her money. Parks looked him square in the eyes, shook her head, and said, "No. That's not right." Enraged by her obstinacy—and doubtless ignorant of its renown—the man began beating Parks, punching her in the face over and over, then throwing her down on her bed and shaking her violently. "I had never been hit in that manner in my life," Parks remembered with a shudder. "I was screaming and trying to ask him not to hit me." Blood flowing from her mouth, the then eighty-one-year-old finally relented and gasped, "All right! Take the money." Her mugger stole $103 and fled. "He could have hurt me much worse," Parks later reflected, "but God protected me." As soon as the thief was gone, the injured Parks grabbed her telephone and called Elaine Eason Steele, who lived just across the street. "It took the police almost fifty minutes to arrive after I notified them," Steele recalled with still a hint of bitterness. Upon the officers' arrival a 911 operator's call was placed, and an ambulance arrived within minutes to rush Parks to the nearby Detroit Receiving Hospital.

Parks was treated for facial swelling and severe bruises, and the world expressed outrage at what had happened to her. Detroit's desperate efforts to reinvent itself as a tourist-friendly "Renaissance City" staggered under this latest outrage heaped upon its reputation for urban mayhem. Parks's neighbor, Moses Mills, summed up the feelings of the community: "Any time we can't protect our leaders, we're in trouble." An angry police chief Isaiah McKinnon snapped, "This is inconceivable. We're talking about a lady who's responsible for changing the course of this country." The assault on Rosa Parks was quickly taken up by editorial writers across the nation, and a truly incensed Bob Herbert wrote a *New York Times* op-ed proclaiming that "there isn't much worse than a society that pretends to be civilized and free while brutalizing its elders and slaughtering its young."

For her part, Parks tried to downplay the significance of the robbery by pointing out that the "sick-minded" criminal who had attacked her was by no means representative of the urban youths she worked with at the Institute for Self-Development. "I pray for this young man and the conditions in our country that have made him this way," Parks responded. "I urge people not to read too much into the attack." That said, the incident prompted her to move out of downtown Detroit's west side and into the Riverfront Towers, a twenty-four-hour gated and guarded modern high-rise complex overlooking the Detroit River just west of Joe Louis Arena, and only blocks from where abolitionists Frederick

Douglass and John Brown met in 1859 to discuss the West Virginia raid at Harpers Ferry. "It's a wonderful safe haven," she said of the new 1,800-square-foot apartment. "I feel very much at peace here."

From twenty-five stories above it, the world looked tranquil to a recuperating Parks as the huge Lake Huron barges drifted calmly down the Detroit River bearing tons of iron ore to unload at the industrial docks of Toledo and on over Lake Erie at Cleveland. Every morning she propped herself up in bed and read inspirational passages from her large-print King James Bible. After rising she made a modest breakfast, downed vitamin supplements, did a round of light calisthenics, positioned herself at the river-view window of her apartment, and stared out trancelike at the majestic span of the Ambassador Bridge to Canada. Whenever a Great Lakes cruise ship floated past, Parks imagined how happy the passengers were and smiled wistfully, wishing Raymond were still alive to savor the spectacular view with her. "Oh, look at that one," she would exclaim to guests at each freighter and tanker in a soft voice full of girlish delight.

Gazing across the river at the skyline of Windsor, Ontario, Parks often fell under the spell of Canada. "That's where Harriet Tubman found freedom," she mused. "Just down the river was one of the most popular crossings for escaped slaves fleeing America." Her new riverfront apartment became Parks's reclusive sanctuary, a quiet refuge in old age from the stormy events of yesterday and the hectic pace of urban life today. In her aerie high above the Detroit River, all was museum-still within the walls lined with precious souvenirs: framed honorary-doctorate diplomas; gold medals awarded her in Sweden and Japan; photographs of Mary

McLeod Bethune, Coretta Scott King, and other personal heroes; and a portrait of Parks herself forty-five years earlier on the infamous bus, a gift painted by her Los Angeles friend Artis Lane. Her china cabinets brimmed with more tangible mementos, the centerpiece a small portable Singer sewing machine she had brought with her from Alabama. Now retired from the seamstress trade, Parks kept the reliable relic handy in case of an emergency calling for a hem.

However, three years after moving into the Riverfront Towers, Parks sustained another shock that pained her even more than her own beating by a deranged hoodlum. In July 1997, the Institute for Self-Development's chartered Rite Way bus was retracing the Underground Railroad with twenty-eight youths and six chaperones aboard when the driver suddenly swerved off Interstate 95 south of Petersburg, Virginia, sending the bus sliding on its side down a 150-foot embankment and into the murky, 5-foot-deep Nottoway River. Many of the passengers were injured—the driver and four of the students, one in a coma, seriously—and twenty-five-year-old chaperone Adisa Foluke, Elaine Eason Steele's nephew, was killed. Parks was devastated. "He was just as close to me as if he were my own grandson," she said of Foluke. "I felt that way about him, and that's how he felt about me."

Harriet Tubman used to brag, "I never ran my train off the track and I never lost a passenger," and now Parks could not say the same. She had not been on the bus, but as the tour's organizer she felt responsible for what had happened as well as heartbroken over the death of her young friend. She flew to Virginia to embrace and pray with the hospitalized students, and to encourage the rest to continue their journey.

Accidents, pain, and death were all part of life, Parks told them; courage meant refusing to give in to despair and marching on no matter what. This was the quiet strength that Parks was famous for, and that she had set up her institute to teach. As unnerved as she was by the catastrophe herself, she told the press, "I'm just hoping . . . that the young people who survived will continue with the program."

Left to decide for themselves what to do, the students agreed with Parks that it would be wrong to quit, and opted to resume their four-thousand-mile trek through fifteen states and twenty-two cities to honor their lost comrade Adisa Foluke. When *Jet* magazine interviewed several of the students for a story on the crash, the group's decision to go on after attending the Detroit funeral was explained by eighteen-year-old Makia Gibson. "I have to, now," he told the reporter. "I have to finish. Until we cross the river into Toronto, Canada, our program says we are not free. We have to press on for our freedom." The students finished the program together, refusing to let the tragedy derail their spirit. "They were brave and heroic," Parks said. "I love them all."

Although she had traveled extensively throughout the United States on the lecture circuit as well as on Pathways to Freedom rides, the only foreign countries Parks had visited before she turned eighty were Canada and Mexico, in each case to pick up an award. But her passport would get another stamp shortly after she met Dr. Daisaku Ikeda, a leading Buddhist philosopher, poet, and educator, in 1992. As president of Tokyo's Soka University, Ikeda had invited Parks to visit its American campus, situated on more than five hundred acres in the Santa Monica Mountains west of Los Angeles, and she had accepted. Over the years Parks had taken an increasing interest in the ethereal spirituality of Buddhism, and she immediately formed a bond with her fellow human rights activist from Japan. "In his concern for human rights, Dr. Ikeda was ahead of many people in this century," Parks would write in Marvin Heifeman and Carole Kismaric's book of historical photographs, *Talking Pictures*, adding that the shot shown of her clutching his hands was one of the most important she had ever had taken. "He is a calm spirit," she wrote, "a humble man, a man of great spiritual enlightenment."

During her visit to California, Parks and Ikeda eagerly discussed new strategies for building a global grassroots movement to spread the philosophy of nonviolence. It seemed to make sense to start with the more than 12 million members from 128 countries of the Soka Gakkai International organization, of which Ikeda was president. Thus it was that in May 1994 Parks found herself on a commercial airliner headed to Tokyo with a delegation of Japanese and Americans to meet her host. Together the delegation ate sushi at the Ikeda residence and toured Soka University's main campus, where eight thousand students lined the streets to pay homage to the "wise serenity" of the "Mother of the Modern Civil Rights Movement." At another event one thousand Japanese students sang to her in English "We Shall Overcome." Her sojourn in Japan opened Parks to the harmony of Buddhist meditation, which she would add to her lifelong Christian prayers as an integral part of her life. The trip proved the most memorable of her life; Rosa Parks adored the Japanese people, and they her. The humility that tempered her matriarchal presence charmed even the Japanese media, which described her as a "great spirit" and a "natural Buddhist" who deserved to be made an honorary citizen of their nation. Japanese translations of Parks's books, *My Story*, *Quiet Strength*, and *Dear Mrs. Parks: A Dialogue with Today's Youth*, quickly became popular best-sellers in Tokyo.

The first of these books had come out in the United States in 1992. To assist her on that initial literary project she had chosen Jim Haskins, an Alabaman and the author of more than eighty books, including *The Cotton Club*, a narrative set during the Harlem Renaissance that was made into a popular movie. Haskins tape-recorded interviews with Parks in Detroit as well as on trips to Mexico, New York, and Gainesville, Florida, and these tapes—which someday will become part of the Haskins Collection at Boston University—are without question the most comprehensive primary source of information on her life. Only a portion of the material from these interviews was used in *My Story*, however, in part because the autobiography was aimed at adolescent readers but also because Parks insisted on keeping some personal anecdotes and private observations off the record as long as she was alive.

My Story was well received, and its success convinced Parks to publish her second work, *Quiet Strength*, an eighty-nine-page pocket book of inspirational stories, prayers, and anecdotes compiled by her attorney and close friend, Gregory J. Reed. "Mrs. Parks and I completed *Quiet Strength* in forty days and forty nights," Reed recalled, "and I'll never forget handing over the advance check to her. It was the first real money she ever made. 'Could you believe it?' she said. And I said, 'Mrs, Parks, you're worth more than that.'"

Shortly after banking that check, in April 1995, Parks presented President Bill Clinton with a one-of-a-kind leather-bound edition of *Quiet Strength* in Sacramento during a session of the California Democratic Assembly. The previous year the president's mother, Virginia, had died, so Parks thoughtfully inscribed the volume in her memory. "May God bless her in Heaven," she said, holding his hand. The startled president just stared at her, fighting back tears. "Thank you, Mrs. Parks," was all he could manage, his voice quaking with emotion.

Aimed at the same teenage audience as its predecessor, *Quiet Strength* focused more directly on old-fashioned advice for young people: Embrace tolerance, avoid drugs, act courteously toward elders, and always do your homework. "I am motivated and inspired by young people and children," Parks wrote. "My eyes light up whenever children come around." And youngsters from all over the world loved Rosa Parks back: Entire classrooms of children often sent her boxes of crayon drawings, pen-pal letters, and trinkets they had made themselves. She received so many letters, in fact, that Reed convinced her to publish *Dear Mrs. Parks: A Dialogue with Today's Youth*, a collection of earnest responses to some of the many children who had written to her. Following the "Dear Abby" model, in her third book, which won the NAACP Image Award, Parks offered her young correspondents advice on everything from eating right to avoiding AIDS, along with her meditations on subjects from computers to the joys of swimming. "People would faint and cry when they met her on the book tour," Reed recalled. "So many people were in awe of her presence and some thought she had died."

In truth, the octogenarian was not only alive but still kicking to do more. Rosa Parks had always been observant enough to look for the patterns in history, to connect events in order to make clear where society's problems lay—and how best to attack them. Even in her later years she spent much of her leisure time reading nonfiction in her Riverfront apartment, particularly works on the struggle for racial equality. Her favorite such books included Morris Dees's *A Season for Justice*, Dee Brown's *Bury My Heart at Wounded Knee*, Juan Williams's *Eyes on the Prize*, David Levering Lewis's *W. E. B. Du Bois*, and every serious work that came out on the life of Martin Luther King, Jr., particularly those by Taylor Branch, David J. Garrow, Stephen B. Oates, and Clayborne Carson. Parks also grew interested in the women's suffrage movement that had sprung from and run parallel to the abolitionist cause in the nineteenth century—after all, its leaders, Susan B. Anthony and Lucretia Mott, had fought for freedom, the vote, and equal rights for slaves and women alike. Parks's interest in the history of the women's movement grew in part from her astonishment at learning that the Antislavery Convention of American Women may have been the first organization in the United States to advocate sit-ins and protest rides as means of nonviolent protest—a policy the women's group had adopted way back in 1838.

Sadly, Parks found more and more time to read as her deteriorating health made it ever harder to leave home. On May 30, 1998, Steele found her lying unconscious on the floor of her Detroit apartment, and immediately called an ambulance to race her to Harper Hospital, where many of her nieces and nephews rushed to Parks's bedside. The strong-willed eighty-five-year-old pulled through, but from then on would need a walker or wheelchair to get around. When she made her first public appearance a month later at St. Matthew AME, the hundred-strong congregation gave Rosa Parks a standing ovation. "We've saved your seat for you," the Reverend Eddie Robinson said as he helped her into the front pew. Her fellow churchgoers felt compelled to touch her cheek, squeeze her hand, and hug her outright. And she did not object, in agreement with novelist Richard Wright that going to church on Sunday was like placing one's ear on another's chest and hearing the unquenchable murmur of the human heart. "If we don't hurry up and elope," Reverend Robinson joked while clasping her hand, "it'll be too late for both of us."

Epilogue

Tell it to your children, and let your children tell it to their children,
and their children to the next generation.

— Joel 1:3 NIV

NOW THAT Rosa Parks's body was too feeble to march and her voice had faded to a whisper, politicians lauded her as a patriotic icon. She had grown as harmless and safe to exalt as former heavyweight boxing champion Muhammad Ali, another African-American rebel icon shrunk by age and infirmity into a shade of a former self, still floating like a butterfly, perhaps, but no longer up to stinging like a bee. At numerous local events politicians elbowed one another aside to get their pictures taken with the honoree—campaign-ready images to signal conscientious constituents, "See? I'm not a racist. Here I am with Rosa Parks." The effect was the same as that sought by the shrewd Las Vegas casino operators who hired African-American boxing great Joe Louis of Detroit to greet customers at Caesar's Palace in the 1960s. Everybody wanted to shake Rosa Parks's hand, but nobody wanted to delve into her lifetime commitment to political and economic justice for black Americans. The myth around Rosa Parks had so usurped her reality as a radical activist that most Americans believed she really *was* just a good-hearted middle-aged seamstress who was simply so tired one day that she refused to give up her seat on the bus home from work. To others, she was no more real than folk figures like Carrie Nation brandishing an ax against demon alcohol or Molly Pitcher risking her life on the battlefields for American independence.

All in all, the 1990s proved difficult for Parks physically and emotionally, but neither her activity nor her optimism waned. "Anything positive or uplifting Mrs. Parks wants to know about," Elaine Eason Steele noted. In between accepting honorary doctorates from top universities, she began taking water aerobics classes, compiled recipes for a vegetarian cookbook, and advised the producers at Zomba Records who assembled over one hundred gospel greats for a tribute album in her honor. Influenced by the teachings of New Age physician Deepak Chopra of India—with whom she collaborated on an audiotaped book—she eschewed traditional drugs and embraced holistic medicine. When Nation of Islam leader Louis Farrakhan began organizing his Million Man March of African Americans in Washington, D.C., many civil rights veterans were at first skeptical. Parks, however, saw the event as a mass rally for spiritual reconciliation and wrote Farrakhan a strong letter of support. He, in turn, sent it out as a press release to newspapers worldwide, thereby garnering an unexpected wave of feminist support for his cause. And when the Atlanta-based rap duo Outkast included a cut titled "Rosa Parks" on their Grammy-nominated 1998 album *Aquemini*, Parks sued, arguing that Outkast had no right to use her name to promote a song she found vulgar and profane, but she lost the case in November 1999 on First Amendment grounds.

On a higher note, under her leadership the Parks Institute created a program through which Detroit-area junior high school students made weekly visits to senior care facilities to teach the residents to surf the Internet and send E-mail. Turning the teenagers into mentors forged real bonds among the participants from both generations, just as Parks had hoped. She herself, a skilled typist but uninitiated into the Information Age, became the program's first graduate in 1998, allowing one Thaijuan Williamson, a fourteen-year-old from Detroit, the lifelong honor of boasting that he taught Rosa Parks how to use a computer. "It's by far the highlight of my life," he enthused. "She was quick to catch on."

Meanwhile, the tributes—thanks to the tireless advance work of Willis Edwards, the Institute's planning director and NAACP National Board member—piled up: The Smithsonian Institution commissioned a bust in her likeness by Artis Lane for permanent display in the nation's capital; on June 6, 1999, President Bill Clinton presented her with a congressional medal for lifetime achievement in facing down racial discrimination; the legendary Morris Dees of the Southern Poverty Law Center created a new "Teaching Tolerance" initiative with her as cochair; and the city of Montgomery, in conjunction with its local Troy State University, announced that on December 1, 2000, the Rosa Parks Museum and Library would open on the very corner where its namesake had been arrested exactly forty-five years earlier. But the pinnacle of Parks's elder years had come in 1990, with the release from prison and subsequent political ascendance of the anti-apartheid leader who would win a share of the 1993 Nobel

Peace Prize and the presidency of South Africa a year later: Nelson Mandela, only five years her junior and thus part of the same graying generation of black freedom fighters around the world. Parks had admired Mandela over the decades, through every phase of his career from headstrong activist to imprisoned idealist to skillful geopolitician. "He is my symbol of hope," she proclaimed. "He is our future."

Just four months following his release after spending twenty-seven years in the Robben Island prison for sabotage, Mandela had set out on a mission to make sure the United States would not lift its economic sanctions against still-segregated South Africa. When he arrived in New York in June 1990 to begin an eleven-day, eight-city American tour, Mandela was feted with an ecstatic ticker-tape parade down Broadway in the glow of an Empire State Building lit up in the green, black, and gold of the African National Congress flag. As the *New York Times* noted, his visit "touched and energized black Americans as much as anything since the height of the civil rights era." And after meeting with President George Bush and addressing the U.S. Congress in Washington, D.C., Mandela headed to Michigan. "It's funny about Detroit," the Reverend Jesse Jackson told a television reporter who asked about the great man's planned stop in the Motor City, where he was scheduled to visit the Ford Motor River Rouge complex and then attend a rally at forty-nine-thousand-seat Tiger Stadium. "It's the home of Joe Louis, and Nelson Mandela has always admired Joe Louis," Jackson explained. "He's also always wanted to see Rosa Parks, and she is here."

Somehow, though, the local planning committee—composed of Detroit ward heelers and businessmen—had neglected to invite Parks to greet South Africa's legendary black nationalist leader when he arrived at the city's Metropolitan Airport. Elaine Eason Steele tried desperately to get her added to the VIP list, but to no avail. "I just shouldn't be there," Parks concluded. "It's okay. They just forgot me." Refusing to give up, Steele finally telephoned Parks's friend, Judge Damon Keith, who declared: "Don't worry about a thing." True to his word, he arranged for Parks to stand at the front of the receiving line, despite her protesting, "It's not proper. They don't need me." Keith told her to "hush up"— if anyone deserved to be there to greet Nelson Mandela, it was the Mother of the Civil Rights Movement.

When the day came, Parks and Keith arrived at the airport with Elaine Eason Steele to find a huge throng gathered for a glimpse of the great South African freedom fighter. ANC flags sprouted everywhere, and vendors strained to keep up with the brisk demand for Mandela T-shirts. Parks, always uncomfortable in crowds, grew nervous as Keith and Steele escorted her onto the tarmac just as the plane arrived. "He won't know me," Parks kept repeating, embarrassed that she had come.

Moments later the airplane's door opened and Nelson Mandela, accompanied by his then-wife Winnie, appeared and waved to the enthusiastic crowd shouting, "Viva Nelson!" and "Amandla!" the Swahili word for "power." Slowly he made his way down the steps and toward the receiving line. Suddenly he froze, staring openmouthed in wonder. Tears filled his eyes as he walked up to the small old woman with her hair in two silver braids crossed atop her head. And in a low, melodious tone, Nelson Mandela began to chant,

"Ro-sa Parks. Ro-sa Parks. Ro-sa Parks," until his voice crescendoed into a rapturous shout: *"Ro-sa Parks!"*

Then the two brave old souls, their lives so distant yet their dreams so close, fell into each other's arms, rocking back and forth in a long, joyful embrace. And in that poignant, redemptive moment, the enduring dignity of the undaunted afforded mankind rare proof of its own progress.

BIBLIOGRAPHICAL NOTES

THE IDEA to write a biography of Rosa Parks first came to me in April 1997, when I took ten Louisiana high school teachers and twenty of their students on a two-and-a-half-week Majic Bus civil rights tour of the South. Sponsored by the University of New Orleans, the program is designed to pique interest in the history of the struggle for racial equality in America. The tour groups discuss the assassination of Martin Luther King, Jr., with the Reverend Samuel Kyles at the Lorraine Motel in Memphis; spend time with Daisy Bates at her home in Little Rock; march across the Edmund Pettus Bridge in Selma with the Reverend Hosea Williams; tour Atlanta's Sweet Auburn district with Julian Bond; and meet with members of the SCLC and SNCC in Birmingham. In Montgomery the Majic Bus visits such heroes of the 1956 boycott as Johnnie Mae Carr and the Reverend Robert Graetz. But the Alabama civil rights icon whose story captivates the students most is Rosa Parks, even though she now lives in Detroit, overseeing the similar "Pathways Toward Freedom" road course.

One afternoon, as I was preparing a lecture about Parks's career to deliver in the courtyard of the Cleveland Courts housing project where she had once lived, I discovered that no serious biography had yet been written of Rosa Parks—only a few illustrated children's books spinning her life as a morality tale. There was also, of course, the worthy *Rosa Parks: My Story* (New York: Putnam, 1992), a fine autobiography for young adults, but it naturally lacked the neutral historian's perspective. And Parks's other two books—the Christian meditation *Quiet Strength,* with Gregory J. Reed (Grand Rapids, Mich.: Zondervan Publishing House, 1994), and the collection of correspondence with children *Dear Mrs. Parks* (New York: Lee and Low Books, 1996)—were not intended as historical biographies. So when the opportunity came to write a volume for the Penguin Lives series, I immediately chose Rosa Parks as my subject.

Because Parks is still alive, getting to know her became a top priority; as she is an octogenarian grappling with declining health, however, interviewing her is not an easy proposition. But thanks to the courtesy of four stalwarts of the Rosa and Raymond Parks Institute—Elaine Eason Steele, Willis Edwards, Gregory J. Reed, and Anita Peak—I did get to spend quality time with Parks in Washington, D.C., Detroit, and Los Angeles. When I finished a first draft, my subject graciously acceded to another interview in California to fill in some missing gaps, which helped flesh out her portrait and added colorful new details to the narrative. I also tracked down long-forgotten interviews Parks gave in the 1960s at Howard University and for Pacifica Radio. The Parks Institute also assisted in setting up interviews with Mamie Bradley, John Conyers, Julia Coleman, Damon Keith, and Eddie Robinson, who provided invaluable contributions to the oral history that constituted a major part of my research. Sandra Polizos of Alabama PBS took me to visit the home of Virginia and Clifford Durr and provided primary source material relating to that extraordinary couple. Over the course of two years I also gathered insights from interviews with Julian Bond, Lila Cabbil, Barbara Campbell, James Farmer, Nelson Mandela, Kofi Annan, Ossie Jefferson Corley, Mary Chambers, William Gibbons, Jim Parker, Fred Burton, Orie Carter, Johnnie Mae Carr, Dick Gregory, Strom Thurmond, Claudette Colvin, Colin Powell, Morris Dees, Fred Gray, Rufus Lewis, Robert Graetz, Daisy Bates, Frank Johnson, and Rita Dove, among dozens of others. When I tried to interview James Blake, the bus driver, he cursed me in a racist rage.

Bibliographical Notes

The wonderful oral history volume *My Soul Is Rested: Movement Days in the Deep South Remembered* (New York: G. P. Putnam's Sons, 1977), edited by Howell Raines, includes seminal interviews with Rosa Parks and other key players in the boycott saga.

The city of Montgomery remains home to most of the surviving bus boycott veterans, many of whom proved eager to share their personal war stories about those 381 historic days. I often attended services at the Dexter Avenue Baptist and First Avenue Baptist Churches to meet Montgomerians who had participated in the landmark protest, and regular lunch chats with locals at Martha's on Sayre Street over some of the best soul food in Alabama afforded me a better understanding of those heady months that had catapulted Martin Luther King, Jr., from obscurity to international prominence.

Forty-odd miles south of Montgomery, in the tiny hamlet of Pine Level where Parks grew up, I talked to old-timers who remembered her as a shy, demure little girl. Crucial insights and details on her later personal life came from numerous anecdotes about "Aunt Rosie" provided by most of her thirteen nieces and nephews. Particular thanks are due Parks's nephew Sylvester McCauley, Jr., her niece Elaine Bridgeforte, and her cousins Thomas Williamson, Jr., and Carolyn Green, whose recollections helped clarify my subject's forty-five years in Detroit.

Oral histories are of course spotty by nature, so a great deal of archival research was called for as well. The Rosa L. Parks Papers, housed at the Walter Reuther Archives of Labor and Urban Affairs at Detroit's Wayne State University, although somewhat disorganized, cluttered with irrelevant newspaper clippings, proved to be an utterly invaluable trove. One wintry afternoon, for example, I was astonished to discover mixed into the collection the actual longhand notes Parks had taken at the Highlander Folk School in Monteagle, Tennessee, in the summer of 1955, when she was first instructed in the tactics and techniques of civil disobedience by Septima Clark and Myles Horton. The Detroit

Historical Museum was also quite helpful in furthering my under-standing of the dismal 1967 riots.

The superb African-American history library at the Tuskegee Institute offered a wealth of contextual background on the influ-ence of Booker T. Washington, the agricultural devastation wrought by the boll weevil, and the impact of the Great Depres-sion on the "Black Belt" region of the South. The first letter Parks ever wrote King can be found in Clayborne Carson, Stewart Burns, and Susan Carson, eds., *Birth of a New Age, 1955–1956: Papers of Martin Luther King, Jr.*, vol. 3 (Berkeley: University of California Press, 1997). In Montgomery itself, three research in-stitutions proved extraordinarily helpful: the Alabama Depart-ment of Archives and History, the Southern Poverty Law Center, and the Levi Watkins Learning Center at Alabama State Uni-versity, where the E. D. Nixon Papers reside. The Virginia Durr Papers, kept at Radcliffe College's Schlesinger Library in Cam-bridge, Massachusetts, aided in understanding Parks's long friend-ship with the venerable activist and her husband, Clifford. The NAACP Papers at the Library of Congress helped clarify Parks's long activism within the organization. And, of course, virtually everything I learned about the post-boycott years came courtesy of Elaine Eason Steele, who gave me access to the archive at the Rosa and Raymond Parks Institute in Detroit, which includes correspondence from Pope John Paul II, Louis Farrakhan, Deepak Chopra, and Jesse Jackson.

Journalism is the greatest boon to any contemporary biogra-pher, and back issues of the *New York Times*, the *Montgomery Advertiser*, the *Detroit News*, the *Detroit Free Press*, *Ebony*, *Jet*, *Essence*, and the *Michigan Chronicle* proved essential for explicat-ing the tenor of Rosa Parks's times. I also drew on a number of books and monographs pertaining to the Montgomery bus boy-cott, seven of which deserve special mention. The Pulitzer Prize winners *Bearing the Cross: Martin Luther King, Jr., and the South-ern Christian Leadership Conference* (New York: William Morrow,

1986), by David J. Garrow, and *Parting the Waters: America in the King Years, 1954–63* (New York: Simon and Schuster, 1988), by Taylor Branch, contain brilliant chapters on the boycott, particularly as it related to King. Garrow also edited *The Walking City: The Montgomery Bus Boycott, 1955–1956* (Brooklyn, N.Y.: Carlson Publishing, 1989), a vibrant 636-page anthology of articles, interviews, and memoir excerpts that contextualize Parks's historic refusal to give up her seat. Historian Steven M. Millner's January 20, 1980, interview, included in this volume, was particularly useful. Editor Stewart Burns's *Daybreak of Freedom: The Montgomery Bus Boycott* (Chapel Hill: University of North Carolina Press, 1997) is likewise a wonderful collection of documents, including the correspondence between Virginia Durr and Myles Horton. "The Montgomery, Alabama, Bus Boycott, 1955–56" (unpublished Ph.D. dissertation, Columbia University, 1979), by Lamont H. Yeakey, offers useful statistical data on 1950s Alabama. Historian J. Mills Thornton III's landmark essay "Challenge and Response in the Montgomery Bus Boycott of 1955–1957" (*Alabama Review*, vol. 33, 1980: pp. 163–235) is indispensable for understanding the political and economic realities of postwar Montgomery. Thornton has also written a detailed study that will soon be published by the University of Alabama Press, and in telephone conversations helped me better understand the roles of both Parks and Nixon in the NAACP. Finally, Martin Luther King, Jr.'s beautifully written *Stride Toward Freedom* (New York: Harper, 1958), his autobiographical account of what happened back then in Montgomery to ignite the African-American freedom movement, retains its power to inspire.

Over the years a few interesting magazine profiles of Parks have appeared, the most enlightened being Roxanne Brown's "Mother of the Movement" (*Ebony*, vol. 43, February 1988); Lerone Bennett, Jr.'s "The Day the Black Revolution Began" (*Ebony*, vol. 32, September 1977); Eloise Greenfield's "Rosa Parks" (*Ms.*, vol. 3, August 1974); Janet Stevenson's "Rosa Parks

Wouldn't Budge" (*American Heritage*, vol. 23, no. 2, February 1972); and Rosemary L. Bray's "Rosa Parks: A Legendary Moment, a Lifetime of Activism" (*Ms.*, November/December 1995). A worthwhile early take on Parks by George R. Metcalf constitutes a chapter in his book *Black Profiles* (New York: McGraw-Hill, 1968). Two talented *Washington Post* investigative journalists—Walt Harrington and Paul Hendrickson—wrote outstanding pieces on the aftermath of the boycott in Montgomery from a thirty-five-year-plus perspective.

A number of fine monographs have been written about the AME Church that was the spiritual mainstay of Parks's life. The most useful are Howard D. Gregg's *History of the African Methodist Episcopal Church* (Nashville, Tenn.: AMEC Sunday School Union, 1980); Clarence E. Walker's *Rock in a Weary Land: The African Methodist Church during the Civil War and Reconstruction* (Baton Rouge: Louisiana State University Press, 1982); and Carol V. R. George's *Segregated Sabbaths: Richard Allen and the Emergence of Independent Black Churches, 1760–1840* (New York: Oxford University Press, 1973). Unfortunately, not a single full book has been published on the role of the AME Church in the civil rights movement. There is a similar dearth of smart, modern histories of Montgomery. Luckily, Alabama history scholar Wayne Flynt produced *Montgomery: An Illustrated History* (Woodland Hills, Calif.: Windsor Publications, 1980), a handsome coffee-table volume that chronicles the city from its Native American origins through Watergate.

Dorothy Autrey's "The National Association for the Advancement of Colored People in Alabama, 1913–1952" (Ph.D. dissertation, University of Notre Dame, 1985) illuminates the racial strife at the Montgomery Fair Department Store, among other things, and I cannot overstate how useful I found *Alabama: The History of a Deep South State* (Tuscaloosa: University of Alabama Press, 1994), co-authored by William Warren Rogers, Robert David Ward, Leah Rawls Atkins, and Wayne Flynt, in understanding the Black Belt region. Although not directly related to Parks, Robert J. Norrell's *Reaping the Whirlwind: The Civil Rights Movement in Tuskegee* (Chapel Hill: University of North Carolina Press, 1985) is a landmark study of that unique Alabama town. Other helpful studies about Alabama include William D. Barnard's *Dixiecrats and Democrats in Alabama Politics, 1942–1950* (Tuscaloosa: University of Alabama Press, 1974), Virginia Van der Veer's *Hugo Black: The Alabama Years* (Baton Rouge: Louisiana State University Press, 1972), and Alexander P. Lamis's *The Two Party State* (New York: Oxford University Press, 1984). I also drew often from distinguished historian Dan Carter's excellent studies *Scottsboro: A Tragedy of the American South* (Baton Rouge: Louisiana State University Press, 1969) and *The Politics of Rage: George Wallace, the Origins of the New Conservatism, and the Transformation of American Politics* (New York: Simon and Schuster, 1995). And, of course, the late C. Vann Woodward's *The Strange Career of Jim Crow* (New York: Oxford University Press, 1965), long one of my favorite books, does a fine job of explicating the social realities of the South after *Plessy v. Ferguson.*

A number of key participants in the boycott saga have penned worthy memoirs. Parks's best friend, who today is head of the Montgomery Improvement Association, tells her story in *Johnnie: The Life of Johnnie Rebecca Carr* (Montgomery, Ala.: Black Belt Press, 1995). Virginia Foster Durr's wonderful *Outside the Magic Circle* (Tuscaloosa: University of Alabama Press, 1985) grew out of a series of oral histories ably edited by Barnard F. Hollinger; in addition, Patricia Sullivan, who is working on a biography of Durr, shared numerous insights and a couple of key documents with me. The Reverend Robert E. Graetz lays out his extraordinary story as a white minister on the black's side during those tumultuous 381 days in *A White Preacher's Memoir: The Montgomery Bus Boycott* (Montgomery, Ala.: Black Belt Press, 1995); he also provided helpful correspondence regarding Parks. I learned a great deal from Fred Gray's splendid memoir, *Bus Ride to Justice* (Montgomery, Ala.: Black Belt Press, 1995). Likewise, Coretta Scott King's *My Life with Martin Luther King, Jr.* (New York: Holt, Rinehart and Winston, 1969) and Lawrence D. Reddick's *Crusader without Violence: A Biography of Martin Luther King, Jr.* (New York: Harper and Brothers, 1959) are fine reminiscences from eyewitnesses and participants in the Montgomery story. Another indispensable source was unsung hero Jo Ann Robinson's riveting *The Montgomery Bus Boycott and the Women Who Started It* (Knoxville: University of Tennessee Press, 1989). Finally, although factually unreliable, Ralph Abernathy's *And the Walls Came Tumbling Down: An Autobiography* (New York: Harper and Row, 1989) and Solomon S. Seay, Jr.'s *I Was There by the Grace of God* (Montgomery, Ala.: S. S. Seay Educational Foundation, 1990) offer telling anecdotes.

In addition to these first-person narratives, there are a number of solid studies of other players in the Parks story. Four books deal with the jurist on the right side of the legal battle over segregation: Jack Bass's *Taming the Storm: The Life of Judge Frank M. Johnson, Jr., and the South's Fight over Civil Rights* (New York: Doubleday, 1993); Tinsley E. Yarbrough's *Judge Frank Johnson and Human Rights in Alabama* (Tuscaloosa: University of Alabama Press, 1981); Robert F. Kennedy, Jr.'s *Judge Frank M. Johnson, Jr.: A Biography* (New York: Putnam, 1978); and Frank Sikora's *The Judge: The Life and Opinions of Alabama's Frank M. Johnson, Jr.* (Montgomery, Ala.: Black Belt Press, 1992). A joint venture by Tennessee State and Alabama State Universities and funded by United Parcel Service led to the publication of Lewis V. Baldwin and Aprille V. Woodson's *Freedom Is Never Free: A Biographical Portrait of E. D. Nixon* (Atlanta, Ga.: A. Woodson, 1992). Historian John Salmond, meanwhile, produced two indispensable books: *A Southern Rebel: The Life and Times of Aubrey Willis Williams, 1895–1965* (Chapel Hill: University of North Carolina Press, 1983) and *The Conscience of a Lawyer: Clifford J. Durr and American Civil Liberties, 1899–1975* (Tuscaloosa: University of Alabama Press, 1990). Finally, Arnold Rampersand's *Jackie Robinson: A Biography* (New York: Knopf, 1997) ably details the experiences of Parks's hero in the 1950s.

The first book comprehensively documenting the history and beliefs of the controversial Highlander Folk School now located in New Market, Tennessee, is *Unearthing Seeds of Fire: The Idea of Highlander* (Winston-Salem, N.C.: John F. Blair, 1975) by Frank Adams with Myles Horton. Another interesting volume, *We Make the Road by Walking: Conversations on Education and Social Change*, coedited by Brenda Ball, John Gaventa, and John Peters (Philadelphia: Temple University Press, 1990), offers edited transcripts of discussions between two of the best-known educator-activists of the twentieth century. Written with the help of Herbert and Judith Kohl, *The Long Haul: Autobiography of Myles Horton* (New York: Doubleday, 1990) traces the Highlander cofounder's life in the context of his work as director of the school. The most reliable scholarly studies, Aimee Horton's *The Highlander Folk School: A History of Its Major Programs* (New York: Carlson Publishing, 1989) and John Glen's *Highlander: No Ordinary School* (Knoxville, University of Tennessee Press, 1996), both cover the institution's first three decades, from its founding in 1932 up to 1962. Another interesting account of Highlander's impact on Parks—and the Baton Rouge bus boycott—appears in Aldon D. Morris's *Origins of the Civil Rights Movement: Black Communities Organizing for Change* (New York: Free Press, 1984), which discusses how the Citizenship Schools grew from the Highlander idea. Further insights came courtesy of PBS's WGBH-TV in Boston, which shared with me a lengthy taped interview Bill Moyers had conducted with Myles Horton in 1981.

The role of women in the civil rights struggle being a major theme of this book, I gleaned a great deal about black feminism from Barbara Omolade's *The Rising Song of African American Women* (New York: Routledge, 1994), Jeanne Noble's *Beautiful, Also, Are the Souls of My Black Sisters: A History of the Black*

Woman in America (Englewood Cliffs, N.J.: Prentice-Hall, 1978), and Julia A. Boyd's *In the Company of Ministers* (New York: Plume, 1993). The monumental two-volume reference work *Black Women in America* (New York: Carlson Publishing, 1993), edited by Darlene Clark Hine, Elsa Barkley Brown, and Rosalyn Terburg-Penn, also proved invaluable. I found Paula Giddings's *When and Where I Enter: The Impact of Black Women on Race and Sex in America* (New York: William Morrow, 1984) a brilliant synthesis of the battles for both racial and gender equality, and Deborah Gray White's *Too Heavy a Load: Black Women in Defense of Themselves, 1894–1994* (New York: W. W. Norton, 1999) likewise illuminating.

Septima Clark, the South Carolina activist who befriended Rosa Parks at the Highlander School in 1955, offered valuable anecdotes about her life in *Echo in My Soul* (New York: E. P. Dutton, 1962) and "Citizenship and Gospel," *Journal of Black Studies* (June 1980), and journalist Sam Heyes wrote a fine *Atlanta Constitution* profile of her titled "Civil Rights Hero Gets Recognition—Decades Overdue" (May 21, 1987). Historian Joanne Grant's *Ella Baker: Freedom Bound* (New York: John Wiley and Sons, 1998) recounts that fearless crusader's contributions to equal rights in America; like treatment is accorded Parks's two nineteenth-century women heroes in Sarah Bradford's *Harriet Tubman: Moses of Her People* (Magnolia, Mass.: Peter Smith Publishers, 1961) and Nell Irvin Painter's *Sojourner Truth: A Life, a Symbol* (New York: W. W. Norton, 1996).

There were a number of excellent general studies on the civil rights movement, not directly about the Montgomery bus boycott, that also proved invaluable: David Halberstam's *The Children* (New York: Ballentine, 1998); Juan Williams's *Eyes on the Prize: America's Civil Rights Years 1954–1965* (New York: Viking Penguin, 1987); Robert Weisbrot's *Freedom Bound: A History of America's Civil Rights Movement* (New York: W. W. Norton, 1990); Steven F. Lawson's *Black Ballots: Voting Rights in the South*

1944–1969 (New York: Columbia University Press, 1976); and William H. Chafe's *Civilities and Civil Rights: Greensboro, North Carolina, and the Black Struggle for Freedom* (New York: Oxford University Press, 1980). The essential *Encyclopedia of Southern Culture* (Chapel Hill: University of North Carolina Press, 1989)—edited by Charles Reagan and William Ferris—always came in handy.

My understanding of white supremacy was greatly enhanced by reading Grace Elizabeth's Hale's *Making Whiteness: The Culture of Segregation in the South, 1890–1940* (New York: Random House, 1998). For the forgotten role of minorities in the Second World War I read Gerald Astor's *The Right to Fight: A History of African Americans in the Military* (Novato, Calif.: Presidio Press, 1998). Elizabeth Moore's seminal work "Being Black: Existentialism in the Work of Richard Wright, Ralph Ellison and James Baldwin" (Ph.D. dissertation, University of Texas, 2000) is a wonderful analysis of the absurdist tradition in African-American literature. Two books were pivotal in my understanding of the landmark *Brown* decision: Ed Gray, *Chief Justice: A Biography of Earl Warren* (New York: Simon and Schuster, 1997) and Richard Kluger, *Simple Justice* (New York: Alfred A. Knopf, 1976). For Parks's reaction to the Selma-to-Montgomery March I read her introduction to Beatrice Siegel's *Murder on the Highway: The Viola Liuzzo Story* (New York: Four Winds Press, 1993).

A number of books on race relations in Detroit proved useful regarding Parks's adopted home: Leonard Gordon's *A City in Racial Crisis: The Case of Detroit Pre– and Post– the 1967 Riot* (New York: William, Brown and Co., 1971); *Detroit: Race and Uneven Development*, edited by Joe T. Darden, Richard Child Hill, June Thomas, and Richard Thomas (Philadelphia: Temple University Press, 1987); Jerry Herron's *After Culture: Detroit and the Humiliation of History* (Detroit: Wayne State University Press, 1993); Nelson Liechtenstein's *The Most Dangerous Man in Detroit: Walter Reuther and the Fate of American Labor* (New York: Basic Books, 1995);

Suzanne E. Smith's *Dancing in the Street: Motown and the Cultural Politics of Detroit* (Cambridge, Mass.: Harvard University Press, 1999); and Elaine Latzman Moon's *Untold Tales, Unsung Heroes: An Oral History of Detroit's African American Community, 1918–1967* (Detroit: Wayne State University Press, 1994). Renowned record producer Berry Gordy, a friend of Parks's, contributed his wonderful memoir, titled *To Be Loved: The Music, the Magic, the Memories of Motown* (New York: Warner Books, 1994), and Detroit's first black mayor provides compelling insights about his city in *Hard Stuff: The Autobiography of Mayor Coleman Young* (New York: Viking, 1994).

Although virtually nothing has been written about Parks's forty years in Detroit before now, *Detroit News* investigative reporter David Josar has kept regular track of the ups and downs of the Rosa and Raymond Parks Institute. A positive look at the Pathways to Freedom program, Noelle C. Collins's "Rosa Parks Rides On," was published in *American Legacy* (summer 1997), and a heartbreaking account of the bus crash appeared in the August 18, 1997, issue of *Jet* (vol. 92, no. 13). Detailed coverage of the assault on Parks in her home appeared in the *New York Times*, "Sadness and Anger after a Legend Is Mugged," September 1, 1994, and "Hard Times in the American City," September 4, 1994. Information about Parks's lawsuit against rap duo Outkast draws from David Shepardson's articles in the *Detroit News* and a scathing critique by Michael Eric Dyson in *I May Not Get There with You: The True Martin Luther King, Jr.* (New York: Free Press, 2000), which also includes a compelling chapter on sexism in the civil rights movement, "The Primary Obligation of the Woman Is That of Motherhood: The Pitfalls of Patriarchy." Also, Anthony Sampson's *Mandela: The Authorized Biography* (New York: Alfred A. Knopf, 1994) and Susan Ager's "Mandela Embraces Detroit: City Rolls Out Black, Green, Gold Carpet," *Detroit Free Press*, June 29, 1990, helped me understand the South African leader's first postprison tour of America.

I also drew inspiration from a number of novelists, photographers, essayists, and poets who confronted Alabama racism in their works. Naturally, Harper Lee's Pulitzer Prize–winning *To Kill a Mockingbird* (Philadelphia: J. B. Lippincott, 1960) haunted me when writing about the Jeremiah Reeves rape case and Clifford Durr's liberalism. Often I would wander around Monroeville, Alabama, Lee's hometown, and contemplate the grim days of Jim Crow. The underappreciated George Wylie Henderson, a leading African-American voice in the Harlem Renaissance, authored *Ollie Miss* (Chatham Bookseller, 1934), a fictional account of an honest black woman trying to survive poverty and racism in the Deep South. When writing about the Great Depression in Alabama I turned time and again to the classic James Agee and Walker Evans collaboration *Let Us Now Praise Famous Men* (Boston: Houghton Mifflin, 1941). Some of Annemarie Schwarzenbach's exquisite Alabama photographs can be found in Josef Helfenstein and Roman Kurzmeyer, eds., *Deep Blues: Bill Traylor 1854–1949* (New Haven, Conn.: Yale University Press, 1999). Mobile native Albert Murray, whom I have the privilege to call a friend, always inspires me to rethink simplistic notions of race in America. Two of his classic essay collections, *South to a Very Old Place* (New York: McGraw-Hill, 1971) and *Train Whistle Guitar* (New York: McGraw-Hill, 1974), burst with joyful wordplay written with blues cadences and idioms. His fictional character in *Train Whistle Guitar*, Scooter, gets his education along the railroad tracks of Gasoline Point, Alabama.

It should also be noted that Rosa Parks, Gregory J. Reed, and Elaine Eason Steele each carefully proofread my manuscript, offering astute feedback and even catching a few factual errors. And as always, my wife, Tammy Cimalore Brinkley, offered editorial advice, ceaseless support, wisdom, and constant love. My friend Shelby Sadler, a brilliant scholar and writer, offered sage counsel and elegant editing throughout the process of writing this book. My staff at the Eisenhower Center—particularly Matthew Ellefson (my student research assistant for this book), assistant director Kevin Willey, and project coordinator Erica Whittington—aided me in so many untold ways it would take pages to recount. And syndicated radio talk show host Tom Joyner and BET TV commentator Tavis Smiley deserve a special thank-you for boldly leading the national campaign to have Parks awarded the Congressional Gold Medal.

Finally, according to Rosa Parks there are three autobiographies that all Americans should read and that helped shape her worldview: Booker T. Washington's *Up from Slavery* (New York: Doubleday, Page, and Co., 1901); W. E. B. Du Bois's *The Souls of Black Folk* (Chicago: A. C. McClurg & Co., 1903); and James Weldon Johnson's *The Autobiography of an Ex–Colored Man* (New York: Alfred A. Knopf, 1927). And I would also like to thank novelist Ernest Gaines of Louisiana for *The Autobiography of Miss Jane Pittman* (New York: Dial Press, 1971), which tells the story of race relations in America through tape-recorded recollections from a strong-willed 110-year-old African-American woman who was born a plantation slave and lived to witness the Black Power movement of the 1960s. Like Parks, this wonderful character is a wizened survivor who perseveres through every kind of bondage and humiliation and shipwreck to become a touchstone for dignity in her old age. At the dawn of the twenty-first century, Rosa Parks has become America's real-life Miss Jane Pittman, not a saint, but a symbol of the triumph of steadfastness in the name of justice.